QH
368
.L 58
Lewis
Naked ape or Homo Sapiens?

DATE DUE

SEP 19 '74			

Naked Ape or Homo Sapiens?

This is a powerful reply, on scientific and philosophical grounds, to Desmond Morris's book THE NAKED APE. The authors find much wrong with some of the conclusions reached by Morris, particularly over the uniqueness of man, the role of his aggression, and the question of responsibility for his ethical conduct and control over the environment. The book points to the damage caused when concepts derived from basic biology are applied uncritically to man as a moral being.

John Lewis and Bernard Towers put forward penetrating views of man's continuing evolution. They have written a serious, highly readable and well referenced book which will appeal not only to readers of Desmond Morris's famous book but to all who are interested in the past, present and future of *Homo sapiens* as a moral and physical being.

THE TEILHARD STUDY LIBRARY

SCIENCE AND FAITH IN TEILHARD DE CHARDIN
Claude Cuénot, with a Comment by Roger Garaudy

EVOLUTION, MARXISM AND CHRISTIANITY
Claude Cuénot, F. G. Elliott, R. Garaudy, Bernard Towers and
A. O. Dyson

ENERGY IN EVOLUTION
John O'Manique

NAKED APE OR HOMO SAPIENS?
John Lewis and Bernard Towers

CHINA AND THE WEST: MANKIND EVOLVING
Robert Jungk, Ernan McMullin, Joseph Needham, Joan Robinson,
Stuart Schram, William G. Sewell and Bernard Towers

NAKED APE
OR
HOMO SAPIENS?

JOHN LEWIS AND BERNARD TOWERS

Preface to Second Edition by
Bernard Towers

GARNSTONE PRESS

Published by
THE GARNSTONE PRESS LIMITED
59 Brompton Road, London S.W.3

ISBN: 0 85511 170 4

*QH
3L8
.L58*

First published October 1969
Second impression February 1970
Second edition with new Preface July 1972

Printed by The Anchor Press Ltd., and bound by
Wm. Brendon & Son Ltd., both of Tiptree, Essex

OCLC 651675

Contents

contd.

Illustrations

Foreword

The writings of Teilhard de Chardin are marked by a constant and passionate concern for man and his future. They show throughout a great faith in man, and a conviction that mankind, which he sees as an organic and self-organizing whole, has before it prospects full of promise. This conclusion was in no way the result of facile optimism. It sprang instead from a sustained effort to understand the coherence that exists between the christian doctrines of creation and redemption on the one hand, and, on the other, our modern scientific insight into man as the product of, and participant in, a remarkable evolutionary process. Teilhard concluded that man must no longer be thought of as a passive observer of evolution, but rather as an active agent prolonging and developing this world-in-process into a future where the full dimensions of personhood can be realized in and by every individual.

In no sense did Teilhard claim to provide a detailed blueprint for the construction of the future. Rather, he sought to explore and to expound a coherent way of seeing man-in-society-in-nature-in-evolution. He wanted others to take up, correct and enrich his own ideas. He also welcomed the fact that others would set themselves to the same task independently of his own ideas, from different starting-points and by different means.

Thus, in *The Teilhard Study Library* we are not concerned so much to add to the growing corpus of exposition and commentary on Teilhard's ideas as to publish the work of scientists, theologians and others who, whether or not directly influenced in their thinking by Teilhard, nevertheless share his belief in the urgent need for man to find significance in the cosmos and to develop a common humanist credo. For it is by an 'ascent towards the personal' in all states and conditions of human existence, that we act out our responsibility for building the earth.

General Editors   ANTHONY DYSON
                                                 BERNARD TOWERS

Preface to Second Edition

The current re-issue of NAKED APE OR HOMO SAPIENS? gives opportunity
to respond not simply to its initial reception, but also to publications
(by Desmond Morris and others) that have appeared subsequently;
also to refer to the remarkable changes that have recently taken
place in the general climate of thinking about man's understanding
of himself, of his relationship to other animals (primates in particular)
and to the environment in general. In the last two years, more has
been said and written about the environment, and about man's responsibility for Ecology in the broadest sense, than about any other
subject of public concern. It seems likely that these issues will prove
to be the main theme of the 1970's. By contrast, when the history of
the twentieth century comes to be written, we may well find the
1960's referred to as 'the decade of the naked ape': the decade of
aggression, of drug abuse, of excessive permissiveness in sexual mores,
the decade of excuses for aberrant behaviour patterns; also the
decade of rebellion in various forms, including violent student protest
and even more violent reaction on the part of the forces of repression—
and all justified on the theory of the innate aggressiveness of mankind.
That much of value came out of all the turmoil cannot be doubted.
But if the 'trendy apes' of the comic-strip cartoons were the ones who
set the pace during the 1960's, anyone who had the temerity to raise
a protest against any aspect of the with-it trend-setters, ran the risk
of automatically being classified as a has-been or worse.

Dr. Morris's sequel to THE NAKED APE was published in 1969
under the title THE HUMAN ZOO.[1] Its publication was preceded by extensive serialization in one of the most popular of the tabloid Sunday
newspapers in Britain. The sexual and aggressive appetites of millions

[1] Morris, Desmond, THE HUMAN ZOO, London: Cape.

ix

were therein stimulated weekly by pictures of men and women 'naked behind bars', or lying prostrate under the feet of slave-masters armed with whips or umbrellas or other such symbols, or hunched up in zoological crates with wisps of straw scattered around. One reviewer described the book as "an orgy of phallic symbolism of a kind that must, by now, weary every well-read sixth-former". Desmond Morris interpreted even normal heterosexual relations as essentially a kind of status-struggle, which naturally linked sex yet again with the other dominant theme of his NAKED APE, namely *aggression*. It was cleverly written for mass consumption. In my own review of it (*The New Scientist*, 2 October, 1969, p. 38), I described it as giving us "yet another Jekyll-Hyde blend of fact and fancy. The blending (of sex and sadism, science and sense) is skilful enough to confuse the general reader as to just where and when Dr. Morris hands over to Mr. Ape".

Publication of the first edition of NAKED APE OR HOMO SAPIENS? occurred some months before the appearance of THE HUMAN ZOO. It received widespread reviews in both the popular and the scientific press, as well as in journals of philosophy, sociology and theology. On the whole it was welcomed as a healthy reminder that modern science has both far more in some ways, and far less in others, than Morris had so cocksurely implied, to say with certainty about 'man's place in nature'—to use the great title of Thomas Henry Huxley's influential book of just over a century ago. One of our reviewers concluded that, in comparison with the Morris volume, "it will not be a best-seller, but it is more likely to stand the test of time". We are confident that some, at least, of the important points we have tried to make will still be receiving attention long after naked-apery has gone the way of other fashionable fads.

A major point made by some of our reviewers was that our evident *worry* over the possible effects, on the minds and habits of the young, of the works we were criticizing, had led us to write too emotively, and hence with too much defensive bias, unbecoming to scientists. During a subsequent period of two years of regular lecturing to many kinds of audiences, and in discussion with students in many of the universities of England and the United States, I recognized time and again that we had indeed been overly concerned. Of course, powerful, polemical writing, if it is replied to at all, tends to induce in the writer an over-emotional sense of urgency. By some reviewers, this very feature was widely welcomed: they thought it was high time that reputable scientists should publicly say 'nonsense' to some of the ideas being popularly promulgated in the name of science. My discussions and debates have shown me that though many have read THE NAKED APE, relatively few have been taken in by it. People mostly seem to have read it for amusement and general interest, and very few appear to be as concerned about, or as affected by, its impact as we had feared they might be. People often find themselves in varying degrees of mental turmoil about war, aggression and sex: who wouldn't be, in view of the patent absurdity of so many powerful institutions of today, and of so many of their advisors and leaders? But one thing seems clear, at least to most of the younger generation I have met with: in searching for solutions to our manifold problems, they recognize that it cannot possibly be right or sensible, for instance, to follow those *Ten Commandments of Dominance* which Morris solemnly says (THE HUMAN ZOO, p. 42) "apply to all leaders, from baboons to modern presidents and prime ministers", and from which, of course, on his general genetic theory of practical naked-apery as the norm for man, there is no possibility of escape. Many people today seem determined to find a better way, a more sensible and more cooperative way, than the 'dominance-submission' thesis allows. They will not be dictated to by scientific theorists any more than by old-fashioned hot-gospellers. Though one is bound to say, in the light of the strange appeal of current groups such as the 'Jesus Freaks', that hot-gospellers are finding readier audiences in some educational institutions just now than are even the best of scientists and other serious thinkers.

All this is part of a remarkable change of mood that has come about in very recent times in educated western society—certainly in educated society on the west coast of America, which is precisely where 'student unrest' had its origin, and made its biggest impact, during the 'decade of the naked ape'. A major factor in my (to many friends, absurd) decision to leave Cambridge for California at the end of 1970 was that during years of repeated visits for research and teaching, I had felt that here if anywhere would finally be found truly human solutions to modern human problems of immense complexity. This is because California has been like a vast experimental laboratory. *Everything* has been tried, and the people have seen and experienced some of man's worst excesses and absurdities. As a result, one here meets numbers of people who are *genuinely* concerned, people who a) recognise that problems exist, b) recognise that they are complex problems

and that facile solutions are worse than useless, and c) have the intelligence and courage—the straight 'guts'—to do something about
them. The contrast with the general mood of apathy amongst British
students is very striking.

One chapter of NAKED APE OR HOMO SAPIENS? was singled out
for special comment by a number of reviewers, namely the one entitled
'Nakedness and Sensitivity'. A new theory is there advanced concerning the evolutionary role of enhanced degrees of skin-contact. It
is not merely that surface-contact is the earliest of the 'special senses,'
and the most fundamental form of biological communication between
individual organisms, and hence of learning. It is further suggested
(see pages 41–49 *infra*) that it was the very reduction in thickness
and length of man's] body-hair—which is what gives him the appearance of nakedness or hairlessness, even though there is no reduction
in actual numbers of hairs—that was a primary cause of the growth,
in evolution, of the human brain. Sensitivity and the constant use of
sensitive attributes produce the fine anatomical complexity and functional perfection of the human brain, both in phylogeny (evolution)
and in ontogeny (the development of the individual). In that particular
chapter it is argued that the development of delicacy of touch was a
major factor in allowing *Homo sapiens* to evolve from his hairy (in
the sense of being covered with a coat of long, thick hairs) ancestors.

It is therefore of interest that two recent books, by authors who
have previously found themselves in violent opposition on the nature of
the evolutionary process, have developed at some length the scientific
significance of touching as a means of human communication. They
are, firstly, TOUCHING: THE HUMAN SIGNIFICANCE OF THE SKIN by Ashley
Montagu[1] and secondly, INTIMATE BEHAVIOUR by Desmond Morris
himself.[2] We had already quoted, in support of our general position,
some of Ashley Montagu's previous writings in the body of this book.
His new contribution, which agrees well in many respects with the
new attitude towards man displayed by Morris in *his* new work,
represents yet another harbinger of the 1970's change of mood referred
to above. A significant aspect of this movement towards *caring* is
being worked out at places such as the Esalen Institute and the Center
for Studies of the Person, both located in California. In these and other

[1] Montagu, Ashley (1971), TOUCHING: THE HUMAN SIGNIFICANCE OF THE SKIN, New
York: Columbia University Press.
[2] Morris, Desmond (1971), INTIMATE BEHAVIOUR, London: Cape.

centres the implications of the sense of touch for the full development of the human personality are currently being studied.[1]

This old, and yet 'new' for the age, notion of the importance of tenderness rather than of aggression between human beings, is given added strength by the growing realization that the 'lower' animals, too, display far more gentleness, playfulness and creativity than biologists have previously acknowledged. Outstanding work has been done in the field of animal behaviour by Dr. Jane van Lawick Goodall. Her recent book on chimpanzees, studied over a period of years in their natural habitat, is a must for all who are interested in seeing, in better perspective, man's relationships with other primates.[2] It is not only primates that often display tenderness in their behaviour: the Goodall study of groups of wild carnivores in South Africa[3] demonstrates beyond question that even carnivorous nature is not fundamentally 'red in tooth and claw'. That early nineteenth-century view is a naive oversimplification of what is in fact a complex, interlocking and truly cooperative system in the 'biosphere'. There is no false sentimentality in the views of these authors, who seem to agree with the basic thesis of our book, that to be truly scientific one must be objective at a truly comprehensive level, and not try to twist complexity into a predetermined simplistic map based on prescientific philosophical predilections.

It is no longer just a small group of 'cranks' who show real concern for the future of our small 'space-ship earth' and for all those people, animals and plants who 'sail in her'. The subject Ecology is now a burning issue amongst the youth of today. There is surely room for cautious optimism that a way forward will be found. In this volume, published as part of The Teilhard Study Library, we laid especial emphasis on the insights into the evolutionary process that were achieved by Teilhard de Chardin. His name is still unknown, or if known, is still somewhat suspect to a great many thinkers. Delay in recognition is one of the prices of genius (or even of extraordinary talent), just as instant recognition and immediate acclaim frequently indicate a certain superficiality. But by now, nearly twenty years after his death

---

[1] For a popular account, see, for instance, the book by one of the pioneers of the movement: Rogers, Carl R. (1970), CARL ROGERS ON ENCOUNTER GROUPS, New York: Harper and Row.

[2] Goodall, Jane van Lawick (1971), IN THE SHADOW OF MAN, London: Collins, Boston: Houghton Mifflin.

[3] Goodall, Hugo and Jane van Lawick (1970), INNOCENT KILLERS, London: Collins.

and up to forty or fifty since he wrote some of his essays, his writings are beginning to have more and more influence amongst philosophers, scientists and theologians. Space does not permit documentation of the growing corpus of studies on Teilhard. Two examples must suffice: the first, of a book now in preparation, which will consist of the televised (*in toto*) proceedings of a remarkable two-day conference held in 1971 in San Francisco, under the joint auspices of the City of San Francisco and the University of California, with the title *Teilhard De Chardin: In Quest Of The Perfection Of Man*. Herein will be found the reflections of distinguished speakers from the fields of science, philosophy, politics, the law, diplomacy, and theology, concerning the importance, for our time, of the work of this man. The second example is a recent volume entitled PROCESS THEOLOGY: BASIC WRITINGS,[1] which the editor says is "designed to orient the reader into a major movement in contemporary theology. The selections are chosen from American process theology, derived from Alfred North Whitehead, and from writings on the evolutionary world view of Pierre Teilhard de Chardin." Whitehead was a foremost mathematician and scientist who developed a new metaphysics and gave birth to the 'new theology'. That scholarly studies are now to be found relating Teilhard's thinking to his (as others have related Teilhard to Pascal, Bergson and Einstein) is sufficient indication that anyone who wishes to understand the modern world and its further movements towards evolution-in-process neglects Teilhard at his peril. Amidst the welter of publications today one must be very selective if one is to keep one's head above water. It is hoped that the references given in this new Preface will help the reader to select wisely. Additional references are quoted (and listed in the Bibliography) in numerical form, as indicated in the footnote on page xv.

Bernard Towers
Departments of Pediatrics and Anatomy
The University of California
Los Angeles

March 1972

[1] Cousins, Ewert H. (ed.) (1971), PROCESS THEOLOGY: BASIC WRITINGS, New York: Newman Press.

Introduction

The commercial success of Desmond Morris's book THE NAKED APE[1] was one of the more remarkable events in modern publishing. In writing this 'reply' to it we do not wish to detract from the many positive features of what could be called a brilliantly executed piece of popular scientific journalism. Scientific or pseudo-scientific? Pseudo-science has produced works belonging to a certain kind of publishing enterprise rather than a concern with truth. This new profession, well-intentioned though its practitioners may be, often seriously misleads the public. It must bear considerable responsibility for the loss of interest in and respect for real science that is beginning to show itself amongst the young. The main 'message' of THE NAKED APE, as of much else that is written in this genre about the nature and condition of man, seems to us to be symptomatic of a wide-spread malaise of the day. This malaise is steadily eroding those very qualities in our culture that first gave rise to the dedicated search for truth characteristic of the Age of Science. In so many people one perceives increasing cynicism and a great loss of confidence about man and his role. We live in, a fool's paradise if we think that Science will survive in the atmosphere of disillusion fostered by meaningless posturings of 'naked apes'. With the collapse of Science will go the civilization to which it has given rise. The consumer society looks like being rejected by its own younger members. The mood to 'drop out' is not to be taken lightly. Another Dark Age, such as Aldous Huxley envisaged nearly twenty years ago in APE AND ESSENCE[2] could very easily be soon upon us. It is a strange delusion to think that if one writes insulting and pessimistic views of

[1] Morris, D. (36) *The original U.K. clothbound edition is always referred to.*
[2] Huxley, A. (23)
NOTE: *Numbers in brackets at the end of footnotes refer to the Bibliography at the end of the book.*

man (for all that they are currently popular), one will help to shake him out of complacency and prevent the very psychological disintegration that the opinions themselves manifestly encourage. Dedication to this delusion is one of the most disturbing aspects of the hold which a certain style of commentating is rapidly acquiring over the media of mass-communication. It may count as 'success' in the eyes of the world, but what kind of success is it that ends in futility?

Morris attempts to justify himself by protesting his concern for the future of man. But in fact he destroys all real faith in the future by stating explicitly, as do most promoters of this fashionable viewpoint, that man has no future at all. According to his version of what modern science says, there is no doubt that 'sooner or later we shall go, and make way for something else'[1]. This generalization is of course a truism for biological scientists who take the concept of evolutionary change seriously. Nothing is static, change is inevitable, and since biological evolution tends towards increase in complexity and 'freedom', future states can never be wholly predicted. But popular writers on evolution often seem to suggest that all change is fundamentally random and therefore meaningless—a very dubious conclusion in the light of modern knowledge of the evolutionary process. The implication, however, is that *Homo sapiens* is as vulnerable and as futile as the dodo or the dinosaur. It is, perhaps, legitimate for science fiction writers, engaged in making the flesh creep but quite properly demanding, first, the suspension of disbelief that one must accord a writer of fiction, to give full rein to fantasies about the takeover of human civilization by chimerae invented in imagination. They use the 'evidence' of scientific popularizers like Morris as a basis for their speculations. It is this air of respectability that is being currently given to ideas that are basically full of despair—ideas that on their own analysis turn out to be as meaningless as all those others that their authors are adept at criticizing in the name of 'science'—that we aim to expose in this book. Morris envisages the end of man, and hopes his work will help to postpone the evil day. But it makes no difference to anyone who has learned to think on an evolutionary time-scale, or to think in depth about these large and serious problems, whether annihilation is to occur in a minute, in an hour, a year or a million of them. The problem of total annihilation is by definition total, and one is merely tinkering with emotions by endeavouring to prolong the

[1] Morris, D. (36), p. 240.

agony. But in effect this is, he says "why I have written this book, and why I have deliberately insulted us by referring to us as naked apes, rather than by the more usual name we use for ourselves. It helps to keep a sense of proportion and to force us to consider what is going on just below the surface of our lives."[1] He then goes on, "in my enthusiasm I may have overstated my case." If, as we think, that was an understatement we shall endeavour, in this 'reply', to put the naked ape concept in proper perspective. We will try to show that a more profound study of man, and, in the second chapter, a more detailed one concerning Morris's central theme of human 'nakedness', lead to very important conclusions about man's role in the evolutionary process. This process links man inextricably not only with his fellow-primates (and as biologists and philosophers we have nothing against *them*) but also with all the other mammals, all the vertebrates, all forms of living and indeed non-living matter. In our view man is literally made of 'the dust of the earth'. Though the authors of this book approach the subject from somewhat different points of view, yet they are united in their conviction that, when seen in proper perspective, our modern knowledge of the evolutionary process gives a much more positive, more dynamic and infinitely more hopeful picture of man's true role than can possibly emerge from the opinion that he is no more than an ape, with no more responsibility (or so it will be thought by many) than befits an ape. Let there be no mistake on this question of responsibility and the current mood to opt out of it. What sold THE NAKED APE by the hundred thousand, apart from the brilliance of its writing, was (a) its provocative and, as we shall show, fundamentally misleading title, (b) the very suggestive "sexy" picture that was used for advertising it, (c) the early parts on sex with passages ripe for quotation in the press, and (d) (on the receptor side) the modern masochistic urge to feel degraded, to welcome disillusion, and to search for 'kicks' as an escape from tedium and boredom. Those who engage in irresponsible action or thinking enjoy a kind of psychological reward, it is true. But the satisfaction achieved by this kind of behaviour-pattern is inevitably short-lived, and in the long term it is always self-destructive. Man must find a way of saving himself from the dangers to which the modern cult of human denigration is leading him. Common sense may not be enough to withstand the pressures of modern techniques of persuasion. It is not more

[1] Morris, D. (36), p. 240.

B

satisfying, nor more agreeable, to end 'not with a bang, but a whimper'. Nuclear weapons are possibly less destructive than the insidious belief in the futility of all things. Courage and hope are what we are most in need of, not least in order to handle the problems of nuclear disarmament. We are currently plagued, to lapse into the vernacular for a sentence, with a host of alternately bullying and whining reporters and interviewers in the media of mass communication, and with academics who fail to see the purposes for which they are being exploited. They say continually, or imply, that man is a nonsense, a sport of blind, irresponsible forces that 'happen' to have thrown up a system that thinks itself capable of self-analysis but which is utterly misled about the significance of its own thought-processes. None of his achievements, it is implied, can possibly 'mean' anything in the long run. All that human achievement can possibly do is to help to prolong, and in some ways to improve the conditions of, an inevitably short-lived survival period. After that, they say, *Homo sapiens* will disappear. The naked ape will vanish, as though he had never been, and with him will inevitably disappear all the knowledge and understanding that he was foolish enough, proud enough, to think that he had achieved. This whole outlook, this whole 'mood' (not always spelled out in so many words) must be challenged. Self-preservation alone (not to mention higher motives) demands that we refute this message in the name of science, in the name of truth. If authors such as Morris, and others we shall mention, prove to be 'successful' in terms other than those of simple commercialism, then *Homo sapiens* may indeed be finished. Their interpretations must not be allowed to continue to dominate the scene.

After THE NAKED APE was published it was given enormous publicity in daily and weekly newspapers, nearly all of which seem to have vied with each other, in recent years, to reach new heights or depths of suggestiveness. Modern man is of course no different from his forebears so far as his keen appetite for sexual stimulation is concerned. Nor is he any different in pursuit of aggressive behaviour-patterns. In previous centuries, anyone who set out to stimulate these baser human appetites out of season was not likely to be judged very highly. Today, however, any criticism on this score is likely to be disregarded: it would be highly improper these days to talk, for instance, of a writer 'tempting' readers to acts or thoughts which, in the modern mood, are thought in any case to carry no stigma, no guilt, and certainly no need for contrition or retribution. Thousands of books, plays, newspaper articles, films and television programmes, have sought to make such things respectable and even to extol them as being more honest. We are encouraged unceasingly to think ourselves excused, so far as anything reprehensible is concerned, on the grounds that we are only acting 'according to our nature' which is bestial. Our 'nature' is defined by reducing man to a plaything of whatever violent elements may be seen in some areas of the evolutionary process. With this kind of backing individual men and women can deceive themselves into thinking they have a right to give way to any kind of violent passion they may feel, and even feel themselves to be justified and virtuous in so doing.

The view that man is solely and wholly determined in his actions by his antecedent history (both his individual, personal history and also his collective, evolutionary history) is a late product of eighteenth and nineteenth century scientific materialism. One of its modern expressions is the doctrine known as Behaviourism. That there is much of value to be learned from study of our past is a view that comes naturally to, and will be continually employed by, the present authors. But there is a difference. The sum effect of THE NAKED APE was to add yet another sizeable plank to the philosophy that has been dubbed 'nothing-buttery'. This philosophy suggests, for instance, that every complex organization is 'nothing but' an amalgam of simpler, more primitive elements, each of which reduces yet again to 'nothing but' a collection of yet 'baser' things. It is well to note the emotion that this sort of argument introduces surreptitiously into the discussion. On the basis of this reductionist analysis everything, in the end, is reduced to powerful, blind, chance forces, which are conceived of as producing and acting on Man as though he were powerless to do anything except add more 'noise' to the general confusion.

In this book we shall subject this general philosophical position to scrutiny in the light of modern knowledge of the evolutionary process itself. We shall also point to some of the more significant features of the evolutionary history of our own species, which is the only product of the process (so far as we currently know) that has discovered anything about the process itself, and has invented general concepts about its nature. But in addition it seems to us important to devote a chapter (see Chapter 2 "Nakedness and Sensitivity") to one particular question, namely that appearance of human 'nakedness that gave Morris the first half of the eye-catching title of his book. We shall be considering later whether it is sensible or correct to look upon man as an ape. But also we want to examine closely the question of his apparent nakedness. What does it mean to say that a creature is 'naked'? Certainly not simply that it has no clothes on, because in that sense all living things are naked. Morris was referring rather to the apparent absence of hair, or fur, on most surfaces of the human body. It is, therefore, to his very inadequate and misleading analysis of the nature and functions of body hair that we want, in Chapter 2, to draw attention. If a far-reaching philosophical outlook is based upon mistaken and misleading analysis of fact, then to expound the fact, is to refute the author. And, in the name of truth and sanity, we think that such a refutation is important and necessary.

John Lewis.
Bernard Towers

CHAPTER ONE

Concerning Human and Animal Behaviour

What is man? In the characteristic tones of those observers of animal behaviour we call ethologists, he is:

> An upright, hairless, ground-living ape, with a swollen head and brain, no snout, rather feeble teeth, a reduced sense of smell, excellent eye-sight, remarkable dexterity and the power of speech.

There has been for over a hundred years—ever since the publication of Darwin's ORIGIN OF SPECIES—a recurrent idea that the theory of evolution linking man with his animal ancestors shows that, after all, man is 'nothing but' a somewhat improved ape; and that the forces of struggle for bare existence, and 'the survival of the fittest', which brought him into existence, are still the basic biological laws determining his manner of life, and his progress, if any.

This was a point of view which fitted in very well with the *laissez faire* theories of the period which saw, as the result of the economic struggle for existence, the emergence of the 'fittest', by which was meant the more efficient, and the elimination of the inefficient, the lazy, the good-for-nothings, the diseased.

Bagehot put it very clearly:

> "Whatever may be said against the principle of 'natural selection', there is no doubt of its predominance in human society. The strongest have always killed out the weakest, as they could. In every particular state of the world, those who are strongest tend to prevail over the other; and the strongest tend to be the best".[1]

[1] Bagehot, W. (3).

With the appearance of a new spirit of social responsibility for the less fortunate, when social evils became intolerable, the theory of *laissez faire*, in this crude form, fell into abeyance; but it still seems to reflect a permanent tendency in our Western Society, and from time to time it reappears, especially in theories which regard man as essentially predatory and aggressive. In his Reith Lectures of 1948, Bertrand Russell spoke of "our largely unconscious primitive ferocity . . . the old instincts that have come down to us from our tribal ancestors . . . all kinds of aggressive impulses, impulses to hold what we possess, and to acquire what others possess . . . inherited from long generations of savages."[1]

But the strongest support of this conception of human nature has come in recent years from those theories which see in man fixed behaviour patterns of aggression, which established themselves in the animal world or in primitive man by their survival value and are genetically transmitted to ourselves. Here they persist and govern human behaviour for the same reason: our survival depends on aggression, and hence the propensity is ineradicable.

These are the views forcefully and eloquently propounded by Konrad Lorenz, Robert Ardrey and Desmond Morris.[2] They all recognize the strong reinforcement which their theories receive from Sigmund Freud, one of whose fundamental beliefs was in man's aggressive nature. In CIVILIZATION AND ITS DISCONTENTS, Freud writes:

> "The truth is that men are not gentle friendly creatures wishing for love, who simply defend themselves if they are attacked, but that a powerful measure of desire for aggression has to be reckoned with as part of their instinctual endowment."

THE HUMAN PREDICAMENT

Now if this type of character were due to the conditions of life in prehistoric ages, or to the imperfect knowledge of primitive man, we could anticipate its gradual disappearance under the conditions of growing enlightenment. But the argument is that this is impossible

---

[1] Russell, B. (44), pp. 20, 21.
[2] The works under discussion are: Lorenz, Konrad (31); Ardrey, Robert (1); Morris, Desmond (36).

because these behavioural patterns are genetically, biologically, determined. They are ineradicable, because they are the product of evolutionary selection and are stamped in by their survival value over a period extending probably to a million years. We have therefore no grounds for hoping that improvement is possible, because the few thousand years of civilization has had too little time to effect any fundamental change in our biological inheritance.

The effect on public opinion of the theories expounded by these authors has been unfortunate; it has deepened the pessimism concerning the human condition, which had already reached depressing levels, and gives little hope for human betterment. This is reflected in many reviews and comments on their books. Anthony Storr in *The Sunday Times* argues that when regarded, as we must be if these arguments are accepted, 'in the same light as other animals', then we are indeed 'inescapably hostile and competitive'. Even an able woman like Katharine Whitehorn finds herself accepting the position, not without some satisfaction.

> "The desire to have and to hold, to screech at the neighbours and say 'Mine, all mine' is in our nature too. Ardrey and his allies have let us off perfection and I for one feel a lot better for it."[1]

Nicholas Tomalin in the *New Statesman*[2] seems not too unwilling to find our ancestors:

> "hairy neo-fascists, wenching, warring and damning the wogs:" their creed "patriotism is enough," "fight for every inch of territory you need for yourself," "hate thy neighbour."

We are descended, he declares, from "jingoistic brutes with the meanness of bourgeois property instincts," well to the right of our extreme conservatives. It follows, he continues, that if these principles are correct

> "Any idea of progress in politics which ignores these ape-like qualities is doomed . . . we are fooling ourselves if we think our aggressive impulses have been squashed."

Mr. Tomalin points out that Huxley, Bernal and Haldane once foolishly supposed that the social environment could improve men if

---

[1] Katharine Whitehorn, in *The Observer*, October 29th, 1967.
[2] *New Statesman*, September 15th, 1967.

it was reorganized on co-operative lines. This has now been shown to be an illusion. The truth, as we can but see it,

"must make, if not reactionaries, at least revisionists, of us all. Man, and consequently his society, is immutable. The old adage 'you can't change human nature' becomes true once more."

We are inescapably hostile and competitive, and the behaviour patterns with which we are so endued are biologically determined and unalterable.

And finally, again quoting Dr. Anthony Storr, who describes human nature as worse than the instinctive behaviour of animals,

"The extremes of 'brutal' behaviour are confined to man; and there is no parallel in nature to our savage treatment of each other. The sombre fact is that we are the cruellest and most ruthless species that has ever walked the earth; and . . . we know in our hearts that each one of us harbours within himself those same savage impulses which lead to murder, to torture and to war."[1]

He adds that this should be a sobering thought to those idealists who desire to work for more brotherly relations between man and man. The idea of a society without strife is a fantasy. "Man's perennial capacity to imagine Utopia is exceeded only by his recurrent failure to achieve it." We are condemned, in the well-known phrase of the philosopher Thomas Hobbes, "To the war of every man against every man"; and to that war there is no end and no peace.

On what grounds do these theorists attempt to establish such disturbing conclusions? The story goes back to Konrad Lorenz whose fascinating books KING SOLOMON'S RING and MAN MEETS DOG have been followed by his latest work ON AGGRESSION, which, in its application of theories derived from fighting fish and geese to man—surely a highly questionable extrapolation—really provides the basis for the theories of both Ardrey and Desmond Morris. Put in the simplest terms Lorenz aims to show, mainly on his observations of the Greylag Goose, that aggression is a basic instinct in all animals which has great survival value.

1   It establishes the dominance of the most powerful males, which by selection produce, care for, and protect stronger

[1] Storr, Anthony (51), Introduction, ix.

young.

2 It spaces animals out over the available ground and thus prevents over-population within the group.

3 It makes for order by establishing the authority of the stronger males, the weaker being ranged in 'pecking order', thus securing 'firmness of social structure'.

As a consequence, "aggression, far from being a destructive principle, is seen to be one of the life-preserving functions of the basic instincts." Lorenz points out the relevance of the authority principle to man: It establishes the permanent authority of the old males, and encourages the struggle for existence in which the fittest survive. We do and must maintain aggression in just this way to obtain these benefits and secure survival.

Does this mean that aggression continues *within* the group? No, says Lorenz, for the strong learn not to destroy the weak. The evolutionary process not only produces aggression but also, necessarily, *inherited patterns of restraint,* or the species would destroy itself. These are displayed in the submission of the weaker to the stronger by making gestures of appeasement. The intra-specific fights always end with the flight or obeisance of the weaker, and the defeated is not killed. This shows how the instinct to dominate and destroy can be modified if the inferiors will learn abasement and submission.

Man can also learn how to survive in spite of this destructive instinct of his. If only the weak will learn 'appeasement' we shall get along very well, and the species will not destroy itself. Let the weaker groups learn to make gestures of submission to the strong and they will save their lives. Then they will arrange themselves in an order of precedence and subordination—what is called, from the study of chickens, 'the pecking order'—the strong at the top and the weaker in order down to the feeblest. The application of the whole theory to man is quite explicit in Lorenz and in those who follow him and build upon his theories. Thus if the powerful will learn to subdue and not to kill—and the weak will learn not to resist but to submit—war and revolutions will cease. Note the social and international implications: If the coloured man is a humble Uncle Tom, there will be no white aggression. If the weaker nation submits to the master race, peace will be preserved. If the Trade Unions put up only a show of resistance to the employers' demands and then display manifest gestures of submission, there will be no class war, but national unity.

LOVE AND HATE

Lorenz also holds that mating too involves what he calls 'the redirection of aggression' by the male away from the female on to another bird. Having satisfied the aggressive impulse, the male now returns in triumph to the female and a sex-bond is thus established. This is projected from the Greylag Goose to man to show that all love is based on and dependent upon aggression and remains so among men —"in every case of genuine love there is a high measure of latent aggression."

Desmond Morris interprets the *pair-bond* in a different way, as being a survival necessity in order to provide care for the relatively long infancy of the primate offspring. But both Lorenz and Morris believe that the pair-bond as genetically established among such animals is the sole basis of marital union and love among men, being inherited from our animal ancestors as a genetically determined behaviour pattern, and appearing everywhere in primitive society.

Unfortunately, primitive man does not manifest this behaviour at all. *The conjugal family*, as we know it[1], is a very late affair. The family begins as an 'extended family' embracing a large number of people, and takes several quite different forms. It continues in one form in India and in other forms in various native tribes. It is clear that these forms are not inherited but developed in a rational way under different conditions, to maintain social unity and secure care for the young. It is reason and experience, not genetical variation and mechanical selection, which determines such patterns of social behaviour among men; and that is why there is not one inherited human pattern of marriage, but an immense variety, invented by men to suit all sorts of special conditions.

Lorenz bases all social cohesion on the sex-bond as it is established in this way. But it appears that the social-bond has nothing to do with the sex-bond. It originates and maintains itself quite independently, and may even be surprisingly weak between animal mates.

Lorenz recognizes however that, although these 'inherited patterns of restraint' necessarily operate in human experience, the

[1] The 'conjugal family' is the simple unit of a man and woman and their children as we find it in our own society.

'ritual of abasement' cannot work if the strong do not see the signals of appeasement. But since modern man destroys his enemy at a distance by rifle and bomb, this genetically formed restraint of aggression is no longer effective, and he is in danger of mutual annihilation.

WHY HUMAN LOVE?

Lorenz endeavours to show that human behaviour of a co-operative or peaceable kind, therefore, must not be seen as motivated by reason or by comradeship, or liking, or love, or ethical codes. The reactions which preserve us from mutual slaughter may take on the *appearance* of friendship or a sense of moral obligation, but they are really based on responses evolved mechanically and touched off by the appropriate signals, not by a recognition of goodness or right, or by a reasoned appreciation of the consequences. Obligation is felt automatically, because it is innate, stemming from "instinctive behaviour mechanisms much older than reason, and not essentially different from the instinct of animals."

Lorenz devotes a considerable portion of his book to showing how the source of love and comradeship, and the feeling of moral obligation, are derived from aggression by the operation of natural selection, and do not involve any recognition of value, or any sense of natural ethic. The argument is that since aggression is the real source of the sex-bond and group cohesion, it is never really absent from them, and never superseded by them. Indeed it is only among highly aggressive animals that the love-bond can appear. "Personal friendship is always coupled with aggression . . . . Partnerships demand powerful intraspecific aggression" (that is to say enmity against others in the group). Aggression can never be eliminated because "loss of aggression would mean loss of territory and weakening of male strength."

Lorenz tries desperately to combine this view with the appearance, through much the same process as that which created the pair-bond, of a group-bond; but the strong impression left is that intra-specific aggression remains except where it is replaced by the submission of the weaker to the strong and the 'ritual of appeasement'.

Is this really true to human experience? Do we naturally hate all our neighbours? Does love really arise from a re-direction of aggression by the male from the female to another man? Is there really no such thing as a sense of values and above all of moral values? Do reason and science compel us always and necessarily to interpret the higher in terms of the lower, to deny the uniqueness and reality of the essentially human by reducing it to what we are limited to on the level of the brain development and conditioned reflexes of birds and fish?

It is interesting to find that further on in his book Lorenz recognizes this, though the whole of his argument for the appearance and significance of human love denies it. For he himself says that evolution creates new values: "An increase in value is a reality as undeniable as that of our own existence". But this would suggest that the recognition of the values of comradeship, of kindliness and generosity, the appearance of a felt sense of moral duty, of the wickedness of cruelty and the significance of sacrifice are unique facts of experience; that like the colour of blood and the blue of the sky they are what they are and not something quite different, purely mechanical, a mere facet of animal aggression.

We sometimes take a masochistic pleasure in denigrating the higher to the lower, in denying the obvious, in declaring that white is really black, and love is really hate, that the material world does not exist, that matter is only mind, or mind is only matter, that man is only a naked ape. Is this sophistication or sophistry? Is it cleverness or stupidity?

The anatomy, structure and corresponding mode of life of both fish and birds differ fundamentally from those of the mammal, and there can be no possible justification for transferring the instinctual patterns of geese to man, especially when it is remembered that the basic brain structure is so radically different as to be quite incapable of the neural processes of even the most primitive mammal let alone of man. When the mode of life, the instinct-patterns and behaviour are so different, it is difficult to concede that geese are likely to provide relevant clues to human behaviour. Lorenz explains this parallel between geese and man as due to *convergent evolution*. But the evolution of small-brained and highly instinctive animals like birds, with very limited means of manipulation and no possibility of becoming tool-using in the human sense, reveals no convergence, but extreme divergence. Man adjusts to his neighbour by intelligent appreciation of means and ends, and by attaining the mental and spiritual level of recognizing and striving for values. We know of nothing approaching this in birds or fish. It does really seem to be a gratuitous degradation of the human species to imagine that the key to its behaviour is to be found by discussing it in the crude terms of fighting fish and geese!

Lorenz is saying little, to us, that is intelligible or rational in treating the behaviour of the goose or the fighting fish as a paradigm of human relationships and values. We have a good deal of admiration for his painstaking ethological observations; but we must reject the extrapolation to man. This is the kind of argument from analogy that invariably leads to error if the alleged parallel cannot be subjected to a crucial test to verify its validity. Enormous damage has been done by social and political thinking—and action—derived by such analogical reasoning concerning theories first developed in biology and then transferred to man in society. Our final word about Konrad Lorenz must be, we are compelled to say—Right about geese, wrong about man!

The Territorial Imperative

Robert Ardrey[1] is a successful dramatist who has turned to anthropology and ethology as a hobby. His theories are based on the observations that birds and many other animals stake out an individual patch of territory and in the mating season defend it against all intruders—for example, *the robin*, who sings not to show his joy or to please us, but to proclaim his ownership and warn other robins to keep their distance. This view squares very well with Lorenz's ideas, particularly with his theory of 'ritual combat' and appeasement, for many animals and birds, when defending their territory, only require a threatening display from the stronger to bring a half-hearted duel to an end before it has really begun. Ardrey sees his instinctive and hereditary instinct for possession as handed down through his ape ancestors to man, and, since "our infant species is not yet divorced from evolutionary process, nations, human as well as animal, will continue to obey the laws of the territorial imperative." Here, then, is the cause of modern war.

Not only is there a fundamental intra-specific antagonism based on this struggle for territory, but in a somewhat curious way Ardrey believes that it somehow provides a bond of unity (as Lorenz

[1] Ardrey, Robert (1) and (2).

does when he derives all social bonds from aggression). Communities establish cohesion on the basis of fierce *internal* aggression. Everybody quarrels with everybody else and these inner antagonisms produce a group of remarkable staying power, which Ardrey calls a *noyau*. It stays together by reason of the creative tension of everyone vociferously hating everyone else *within* it!

Far more significant, because it can so easily persuade people of the inevitability of war, is Ardrey's theory of 'the fight for the homeland'. The human group in possession of its territory will behave according to the universal laws of the territorial principle. What we call patriotism is thus a calculable force which animates man as much as other animals, be they monkeys, lemurs, geese or robins.

"The threat of conquest is normal, continual, and rests on an ingredient neither exceptional nor artificial. There is constant probing of other's territory. Weakness is inevitably followed by invasion."[1] Why do men invade the territories of others? Because "*Men are predators.*"

The aggressive spirit, Ardrey declares, has great survival value. Either we stand and fight or we go under. Only if we are strong enough to fight and conquer do we survive. Moreover it alone creates the bonds holding a society together. *The fiercer the attacks the stronger the amity within.* In fact there *is* no amity within apart from the cohesion rendered necessary in order to stave off attack.[2]

If this holds today we realize that there can be no social feeling under conditions of universal peace. War is necessary if society is to hold together.

Like Lorenz, Ardrey finds in Freud's theory of a basic human instinct of aggression powerful support for his theories. He quotes the following passage from Freud's CIVILIZATION AND ITS DISCONTENTS:

"Men are not gentle, friendly creatures wishing for love, who simply defend themselves if they are attacked; a powerful measure of aggression has to be reckoned as part of their instinctual endowment."[3]

Ardrey describes this as "the last fresh breeze of common sense to reach that dank, many-chambered nautilus, modern psychology," and adds that Freud's view has received further support from

---

[1] Ardrey, Robert (2), p. 279.
[2] *Op. cit.*, p. 270.
[3] Freud, S. (18), p. 85.

the theory that "aggression grows greater if it does not draw retaliation."[1]

Freud regarded this basic instinct of aggression and destruction as the greatest obstacle to civilization.

Ardrey and Morris accept without hesitation the transfer of the aggressive instinct from animals to man.

"I can discover no qualitative break between the moral nature of the animal and the moral nature of man . . . The threat of conquest is normal, continual and resting on ingredients neither exceptional nor artificial . . . There is constant probing. Any sympton of illness, disability, or social instability will be rewarded by invasion . . . A portion of a neighbouring property may be added to the domain of the successful . . . [We have here] an innate behaviour pattern, an open instinct, an inward biological demand placed in our nature by the selective necessities of our evolutionary history."[2]

Nor is there any chance of eradicating this aggressive component of our instinctual endowment—"We deal with the changeless."

African Genesis

How exactly did this instinct arrive in man's ancestors? On this question Ardrey has some surprising things to say, surprising especially to those who know something about man's origins.

The answer to this question takes us to South Africa and to Tanzania where the remarkable Man-Ape (or Ape-Man), *Australopithecus* lived at least a million years ago. Several species were discovered by Dr. Raymond Dart and Professor Broom between 1924 and 1947, and others later by Dr. L. S. B. Leakey. But it was not until Leakey found pebble tools closely associated with the skull of what he called *Zinjanthropus* in 1959, that any convincing evidence was forthcoming as to the capacity of this creature to fabricate tools. With them were also found the bones of animals presumably killed in hunting. Beyond this we have no idea at all as to how these creatures lived.

[1] *Op. cit.*, p. 295.
[2] Ardrey, Robert (2), pp. 78, 103, 279-280.

Ardrey assumes that the first Ape-Men of this *Australopithecus* genus abandoned the pacific ways of fruit eaters when they descended from the trees, and became carnivorous predators, entering upon the stage of humanity as "killers armed with lethal weapons". Hence man, like his ancestor, is by his inherited and unalterable nature "a predator whose natural instinct is to kill with a weapon".[1]

These expressions do not merely tell us that man now eats not only vegetables and fruits but also flesh, they are intended to show us (without any evidence except a few pebble tools and animal bones) that the first men were ferocious, combative, cruel, and instinctive aggressors. This becomes clear when, combining this picture with the theory (also advanced without any evidence as to its association with men) of the territorial imperative, Ardrey shows us man as essentially 'the intruder' invading the territory of his neighbours. In other words the purpose of the theory is to prove that modern man is instinctively aggressive and that this is the cause of his incessant war making.

STRAIGHT AND CROOKED THINKING

In these two books there is rarely any attempt to pass beyond the purely speculative hypothesis. But guesses are not scientific fact unless proven; and matters that have been disproved, as so many of his statements are, cannot be asserted as facts. One cannot but question Mr. Ardrey's competence to deal with material demanding extreme caution, discriminating and accurate statements of comparative anatomical and geological fact—but here Mr. Ardrey is not in a position to help us. As he himself tells us, he "blundered into the field, brandishing ignorance like a coat of arms, not knowing a humerus from a tibia." These are hardly the qualifications we require to reveal the true nature of those ancestors whose predatory and aggressive instincts we are supposed to inherit.

Morris and Ardrey have buttressed their works with a huge apparatus of references. But very few authorities actually appear in the texts, or are quoted directly by way of support. The majority of them are unlikely to share the author's opinions. In fact whatever qualifications Desmond Morris and Robert Ardrey have, these do not extend to familiarity with modern theories of evolution, or to

[1] Ardrey, Robert (1), p. 316.

genetics, on which their whole case rests, or to the fossil history of early man and his precursors—a highly specialized study—or to the study of comparative psychology. This is not to question for a moment the competence of Desmond Morris on the captive Apes of the Zoo, or Konrad Lorenz on fighting fish, geese and other animals. Nor is one throwing any doubt on Robert Ardrey's ability as a dramatist of distinction. But competence in one sphere, however great, does not extend to totally different disciplines. It seems highly problematical that recognized experts in the field of neurology, human evolution and comparative psychology would endorse the the theories so gaily and brilliantly set before us in these books.[1]

---

[1] See Montagu, Ashley (1969), *Man and Aggression*, O.U.P., published while this book was at press.

C

CHAPTER TWO

Nakedness and Sensitivity

THE SCIENCE OF THE REAL

Though there is much of interest and of permanent value in THE
NAKED APE, there is one error so glaring and fundamental that it calls
into question the whole endeavour. It is of the greatest significance
that Morris criticizes only one group of professional scientists, only one
discipline within the family of the biological sciences. His choice is
symptomatic of that curious rejection of the real world, for prescientific or philosophical reasons, that marks what we have called
'pseudo-science'. On at least four occasions (pp. 41, 66, 67 and 69)
Morris is sharply critical of professional exponents of the most basic
or fundamental of the biological sciences, namely anatomy. Anatomy
is the science of the structure and development of organisms, the
science of the real. Once again, Morris here merely reflects and
contributes to current trends, because even in the universities there
have been many attacks on this subject in recent years. Rejection of the
study of real objects in favour of more theoretical and more abstract
concepts about them is bound to be harmful in the long run. Tradition-
ally it has been the glory of science to concern itself with facts rather
than opinion. Facts are hard to acquire, whereas opinion is open to
anyone. Now knowledge of structure, of what a thing is made of, is
indispensable for an understanding of what it does, of its role in nature.
This we all accept when it is a question of some erudite anatomical

study such as the structure of the DNA molecule. Working out the structure of things by using an electron-microscope or X-ray diffraction techniques is more exciting, because of the sophistication involved, than is working out the structure of things by use of the naked-eye or the light-microscope. But if you are studying things in the world of ordinary human dimensions, such as the bodies of men and women and apes, it may well be that the appropriate tools of investigation are the time-honoured ones of ordinary microscope and naked-eye. The fact that you may be repeating observations that were made by others a long time ago in no way detracts from the value of the work, provided that the observations are accurate and correspond to what is really there. To disparage observations simply because they are 'old-hat' is absurd. Just to pretend that a structure *isn't there* or is different from what it actually *is*, is to court disaster, and this is what seems to have happened to Morris with regard to human body hair.

EVOLUTION AND HAIR

Morris is rather condescending about those anatomical scientists who pointed out years ago that man, far from being really 'naked' (devoid of hair), actually has a larger number of hairs per unit area than do other primates or indeed mammals generally. It is not surprising that he tries to belittle this fact, because the general 'reductionist' approach which he adopts always tends to suggest that what little hair man still possesses is just another of those evolutionary leftovers of which we shall speak shortly. Morris reports many theories as to why hair should be a 'regressive' feature in man, but is forced to admit that none of them is really satisfactory. When he comes to the question of actual numbers of hairs the problem makes him pause for a moment, but a well-tried popular technique for handling awkward points quickly comes to his aid:

> "Even so, all adult members of our species do have a large
> number of body hairs—more, in fact, than our relatives the
> chimpanzees. It is not so much that we have lost whole hairs
> as that we have sprouted only puny ones. (This does not,
> incidentally, apply to all races—negroes have undergone a
> real as well as an apparent hair loss.) This fact has led

certain anatomists to declare that we cannot consider ourselves as a hairless or naked species, and one famous
authority went so far as to say that the statement that we
are 'the least hairy of all the primates is, therefore, very
far from being true; and the numerous quaint theories that
have been put forward to account for the imagined loss of
hairs are, mercifully, not needed'. This is clearly non-
sensical. It is like saying that because a blind man has a
pair of eyes he is not blind. Functionally we are stark naked
and our skin is fully exposed to the outside world. This
state of affairs still has to be explained, regardless of how
many tiny hairs we can count under the magnifying lens."[1]

One would have thought that since the very title of his book
is involved, the author would have gone into more detail about what
is in fact, on his own admission, a very puzzling business: why *is* the
surface of human skin 'exposed' to such a degree, and what can be the
evolutionary significance of this fact? And why, on the other hand,
does man have more fine and delicate body-hairs than other closely-
related species have long coarse ones? Racial differences in regard to
the number of hairs are not simply related to climate, as Morris perhaps implied with his remark about negroes, since there are a number
of races in the Far East, especially the Mongols, where the trend we
are considering has gone much further than in Western European
Man. It is highly misleading to refer disparagingly to the short body-
hair characteristic of *Homo sapiens* as being 'puny' or 'tiny' as Morris
does. This is another example of the reductionist's 'nothing-buttery'
philosophy. Use of this technique has been a well-recognized habit
amongst popular writers on the theory of evolution. Their intention
has mostly been to 'dethrone' man, to 'reduce him to the level of the
brutes' for philosophical or anti-theological reasons. Thus it became
commonplace in the nineteenth century to refer to the human body
as though it was 'nothing but' a kind of rag-bag of left-overs from the
flotsam carried down on the stream of evolution. Of course, our bodies
do contain relics of former ages, as is inevitable in an evolving system
which consists of 'descent with modification'. There are structures in
the human body which are tending to disappear—the little toe, for
instance, or (by a curious quirk of popular nomenclature) what we
call the 'wisdom' teeth: people who have minuscule little toes, or who

[1] Morris, D. (36), p. 41.

cut their 'wisdom' teeth either late in life or not at all, are clèarly more 'advanced' from an evolutionary standpoint. But the nineteenth century idea that the human body is full of useless left-overs from earlier epochs is quite misleading. It was a theory developed in the early days of evolution, when the materialist philosophy was in violent reaction against that pre-evolutionary, pious notion that every portion of the human body was specifically designed by an omniscient and omnipotent 'divine watchmaker'.

Although we know much more today about structure and function than we did even ten or twenty years ago, these hoary old ideas about the 'uselessness' of organs in the human body keep on cropping up. How often, for instance, do we read disparaging references of this kind made to the tonsils or to the appendix? These are two organs that form part of the vast complex known as the lymphoid system. As the public has recently become aware, in the glare of publicity surrounding the operation of organ-transplantation between one person and another, it is on this lymphoid system that we depend for combating infection and for developing immunity against foreign proteins. Now man has a very complicated lymphoid system. It may well be that his longevity, as compared to other mammals of comparable size, is a direct result of the efficiency of this particular body-system in man. And yet, until quite recently, people were having their tonsils removed on the slightest provocation. The loss of healthy tonsils was 'justified' on the grounds that they were useless organs anyway, and liable to give trouble at any time. It was thought best to get rid of these left-overs from the supposedly mindless, purposeless swirls in what was regarded as the blind stream of evolution. The same argument is still applied to the appendix. Operations for the removal of this organ even when healthy are still carried out in large numbers. They are carried out without adequate reason, out of ignorance, and as a direct result of the kind of prejudice that comes from inadequate science and the philosophy of 'nothing-buttery'.

Now Morris tries to persuade the public that all those innumerable short, fine, delicate hairs on the surface of man's body are just another left-over, a bit of flotsam of no real interest or significance. When he learns that in number they have actually increased compared to other primates he is sharply critical of those who discovered, described, and commented on this surprising but surely fascinating phenomenon.

GROWTH AND FUNCTIONS OF HUMAN HAIR

Human hair, like that of any other mammal, is a product of the outer layer, or epidermis, of the skin, although its root goes quite deep below the whole thickness of the skin. In the embryo the outermost layer of cells is known as the ectoderm, and little buds of proliferating ecto-dermal cells (the future hairs) begin to sprout as early as the beginning of the third month of intra-uterine life. They push their way through the future dermis or 'true skin' and burrow down like tiny solid rods into the underlying subcutaneous tissues. The deepest part of the rod then forms the future 'bulb', as it is called, of the root of the hair. The hair itself is formed in the bulb, and as it grows its tip is pushed back along the track of the original ingrowth, which becomes therefore a tunnel or socket for the shaft of the hair. The tip of the hair emerges from its 'follicle' (which is what the whole system is called) and breaks the surface of the body, in many areas, by the fourth month of intra-uterine life. It is important to realize that these hair buds, forming so early in life, represent the full number of hairs that will ever appear at any one time in the life of the individual (except for very occasional events such as the subsequent splitting of a follicle into two when it starts one of its many periods of active growth). The total number of hair-buds or hair-germs averages about two million in a man. Since they are formed at a time when the developing baby is only about three inches long, it means that the degree of packing (that is, the number per unit area) is greatest at the start. The hair-follicles gradu-ally spread apart as the total body-surface increases in area. Now two million is a very large number. It should not be possible to ignore this fact, or to try even to disparage it, and hope to get away with subsequent observations or theories on the topic. The fact that the majority of the hairs on the human body are short and delicate rather than long and coarse is, to a scientist, a matter for close enquiry rather than for the kind of dismissal which Morris accords it. It is true that, compared with some body-systems, comparatively little experimental work has been done on human hair, and that much of what we are about to say must be speculative. If THE NAKED APE stimulates medical and biological scientists to devote more of their energies to this im-portant system, it will have done good. But already enough is known about human body-hair to be able to say that Morris's reductionist hypothesis is quite inadequate to 'explain' what it evidently sets out to 'belittle.'

Every hair-follicle, after it is first formed in the fetus, undergoes a personal life-history which consists of successive periods of growth followed by periods of quiescence. The time-ratio of periods of activity to periods of rest is about nine to one. A period of growth follows the pattern outlined above for the development of the first hair: the follicle proliferates down into the subcutaneous tissue, and the actual hair develops in the bulb of its root. The tip of the new-formed hair then pushes its way to the surface, like plants do that grow from bulbs. A growth-phase may continue for months or for years, but it never continues indefinitely. That is why even the longest kind of hair 'stops growing' when it reaches its characteristic length. The hair in each region of the body has its characteristic style and length. In some areas (especially in the pubic and arm-pit regions, and also on the face and chest in the case of men) the hairs change both style and length at certain ages. But in all cases it is the 'same' hair in the sense that it is derived from the same original follicle, but now in a new growth-phase. When in any particular cycle of activity the growth-phase comes to an end, the hair 'stands still' in length, and the root of the follicle shrinks into a quiescent or sleeping phase. During this time the hair may be easily pulled out, or may fall out. This involves permanent loss only if the follicle fails to 'waken up' and start an active phase again. When it becomes active again it grows as before, deep into the subcutaneous tissue, and produces a new hair which grows back up the tube of the follicle. If the old, dead hair hasn't already fallen out the new hair pushes it out as it grows towards the surface.

It is, then, the same follicles, in any one site, that produce each of the different kinds of hair that may develop there at different periods in one's life. On the face, for instance, the first-formed hair in the fetus is the so-called 'lanugo': long, soft hairs that may represent an evolutionary 'memory'. These particular hairs are normally shed before birth, being replaced by the short, soft, downy hair that embryologists call 'vellus'. If the transition has not occurred at the time of birth the baby may present a disturbing, even frightening appearance. But there is really no cause for alarm, since the next growth-phase of the follicles will produce the 'right' kind of hair on the baby's face. This 'vellus' hair is characteristic of the body generally, as well as of chin, cheeks and forehead of children and women. Male sex hormone, starting to circulate in the blood-stream at puberty, stimulates the same follicles on cheeks and chin, when they enter a new growth-phase, to produce the coarser and longer type of hair that makes up the beard. Such changes in the character of hair can take place, in certain regions of the body, in both men and women and at any age. They largely depend on the type and concentration of the hormones that are being produced by the different glands of the body. The appearances that result give doctors important information about the normal or abnormal functioning of glands including the sex-glands. There is a hormonal background to some types of baldness, just as there is to some types of excessive hairiness. After middle age it is very common to find that the follicles just inside the ears and nose, which previously produced fairly fine hair, now start to produce much longer and coarser hair. Clearly there are functional differences between the types of hair developed in different regions of the body. For instance, the functional significance of long head hair is almost certainly adornment, providing for the 'sexual selection' that Darwin correctly argued was a potent factor in the evolutionary process. The special sex hair, in the pubic and axillary (armpit) regions, probably acts in retaining the secretions of the special glands in the regions concerned. These secretions can act as powerful smell aphrodisiacs. The importance of smell in stimulating sexual appetites has long been recognized in man, and has led to powerful industries devoted to perfumes. Direct stimulatory effects of special smell glands around the genitalia have recently been proved experimentally in higher primates. On all this kind of topic Morris can be read with interest and profit. It is because he deals so inadequately with the nature and function of our normal, delicate body-hair that his book and especially its title stand condemned as unscientific.

SKIN SENSITIVITY AND HUMAN BEHAVIOUR

Anatomically-speaking human skin is extraordinarily rich in its supply of nerves. The association of a very sensitive skin with the largest central nervous system ever produced in any animal group is by no means fortuitous. It is not only the epidermis that is developed from the embryonic ectoderm, as described above. The brain and spinal cord, and all the nerves of the body are also derived from the same cells of the embryo. Knowledge of early stages in embryological development can give a great deal of insight into adult arrangements and correlations. In science we look for correlations between phenomena, and then create hypotheses that will either give a rational and testable explanation of the correlation or else expose it as simply fortuitous. In the course of evolution *Homo sapiens* has developed a remarkable brain, so remarkable that it has given him his name. He has also developed a remarkable skin, which constitutes the largest sense organ of the human body. This is no chance affair. Human brain and human skin are not unrelated variables, either of which might equally well have 'turned up' in any other zoological group, as the advocates of meaninglessness often seem to imply. Without the one we could not have had the other, and vice-versa. That is not to say that no other option was open to living matter in its evolution of complexity-consciousness: one can imagine other sensitive systems giving rise to high levels of conscious awareness. But given man's inheritance from the primate stock, given his membership of the mammalian class and the vertebrate phylum, it is clear that brain and skin are intimately linked, and inevitably linked, both in origin and function. If a man is experimentally deprived of all sensory input through his skin he quickly becomes disoriented. Doctors have recognized throughout the centuries that there is a close correlation between nervous and skin disorders. The emotional impact and significance of the human touch-sense is well recognized by Morris himself, who draws attention to the extreme sensitivity of most people to accidental skin-contact. The joys and satisfaction of mutually-sought and shared skin-contact are obvious enough. We all know these things (as pleasant, if we are lucky) from our personal experience of this boundary-layer between the 'me' and the 'not-me'. For all that special sense organs like eyes and ears are very important, it is true to say that skin is our basic and principal means of communication with the environment. Whether we experience this boundary-region primarily as a closed door that protects us from a hostile world, or rather as an open one that connects us with a friendly world, probably depends, like so many things, on the extent to which we learned, as infants, to respond to the kind of handling we received from the particular mother or 'mother-figure' that we were lucky enough, or unlucky enough, to be given. If modern psychology has discovered anything with reasonable certainty, it is that infants and children positively need, if their potential is ever to be actualized, the love, security and care that most parents tend naturally to give them. A baby's experience, through its skin, of being fondled and caressed, appears to be vital for its subsequent psychological development. It may be we are just now reaping the results of the popular prewar mood for 'toughness in handling', and 'feeding by the clock' that was promoted by so-called experts in baby-care. A baby's tactile experience possibly determines, or helps to shape at any rate, its subsequent competence in the field of personal relation-ships: love and tolerance, for all their seeming rarity in the modern world, are not only the most ennobling of virtues but are also the most characteristically human of behaviour-traits.

Since man is so plastic in his behaviour-patterns, since he is so responsive to the environment in which he is placed, especially in early years, those of us who are really concerned about man's welfare and future should surely concern ourselves primarily, as scientists, with trying to understand how these peculiarly human traits emerge, and how they can be encouraged to develop. It is not more realistic to emphasize only that from which we have come. It is not merely idealistic to pay attention also to the potential that is in us. Common sense demands that we look at both, our past and our possible futures.

The potential that is given us by the structural link between skin and brain is enormous, and we do well to study methods of actualizing it. It is surely not by chance that we speak metaphorically of insensitive people as 'thick-skinned'. Men with long, coarse hairs on their bodies are thought of as being especially tough, masculine and aggressive. And women sometimes go to extraordinary lengths to hide the fact that their arms and legs are covered with delicate hairs. The link that exists between skin and hair on the one hand, and intel-lectual and emotional sensitivity on the other, has been a crucial one in the evolutionary development of *Homo sapiens*. If we want to try to understand our place in nature and our possibilities for the future, we cannot afford to ignore this link or to misinterpret it.

All living matter is sensitive in that it will react to environ-ment stimuli. According to behaviourist dogma living matter is *only* reactive, and reacts only to restore an inner equilibrium which is essentially inactive and passive. For half a century this negative, nonexploratory and pessimistic outlook has had great influence in biology. But now we are beginning to see that living matter, while wholly material in its composition—and perhaps it is worth pointing out that neither the christian nor the marxist author of this book has any time for immaterial 'ghosts' imported into human machines—has the property and power of actively seeking, learning and *doing* things. Whenever, and in whatever way, we see such powers manifesting themselves, we can either try to 'explain them away' on a 'nothing but' hypothesis, or we can accept them as examples of the potentialities of matter-in-duration—that is, of matter in evolution. The latter approach, and the investigations it gives rise to, constitute real science, and are constructive, as against the former approach, which is ultimately destructive. We, for our part, wholeheartedly affirm the value of being. This is not simply an emotive statement. It is the result of our analysis of how things are, how they have come to be through the evolutionary process, and how they could be if we only took the evolutionary hypothesis seriously and extrapolated its meaning into the future as a basis for action.

The apparent nakedness of *Homo sapiens*, when seen in an evolutionary setting and in the light of his astonishingly complex central nervous system, has great significance. Skin has become, in man more than in any other animal, a vast receptor-organ for information from the environment. In so doing it has lost some of its ancient protective qualities, such as hard scales, coarse dense hair, and sheer thickness. But the gains have been immeasurably worth-while, because increased receptivity means increased awareness and freedom. We no longer need heavy biological armour-plating to stay alive, because our brains have made us smart enough to defend ourselves intelligently (mainly, it should be noted, by evasive action). We are, of course, smart enough to construct offensive weapons too, and man has been doing this from time immemorial. But if objective analysis of the evolutionary trends that have led to man tell us anything at all with abundant clarity, it is that his intellect and sensitivity, his ability to love and work for his fellows, his quest for happiness—and his experience of finding it only when he manages to transcend selfish interests— all are features that should allow us to point to a possible future ahead where, through hard work and resolute adherence to the system we are beginning to understand, man's potential could conceivably be achieved. Looking ahead and aiming at a goal are integral to man's evolutionary prospects. Looking back at where we came from can provide a further source of optimism. But, in the hands of so many writers and commentators today, looking back has become an excuse for opting out of living and for making do with mere diversion. If man fails, it will be through boredom with the consumer society. We need a new goal, and more and more people are finding that goal in the writings of Teilhard de Chardin. For that reason we are publishing this book in the series associated with his name.[1]

NERVES AND SKIN

Let us look, therefore, at the innervation of human body-hair, and also at the innervation, in man, of the relatively few truly hairless or naked regions of the body. There are basically three different types of cutaneous nerve-endings concerned with the input of information. If one is going to 'feel' anything through the skin these nerve-endings must be stimulated, and the nerve pathway between the ending and the areas of the brain associated with conscious appreciation must be intact and functional. The stimulus must occur while the system is in a condition to respond, if it is ever to be 'appreciated' consciously: there are ways of blocking the response, either by exhaustion after repeated stimuli, or by so modifying the whole receptor system, as in conditions of extreme excitement or stress, that a stimulus is simply ignored. The three types of nerve ending are (a) so-called 'free' nerve endings, where the fine peripheral branches of the nerve-fibres ramify freely amongst the cells of the epidermis, (b) 'encapsulated' nerve endings, which lie close to the under-surface of the epidermis and are possibly concerned with the reception of special stimuli such as temperature-differences and pressure, and (c) nerve endings ramifying round the roots of the hairs, about which we shall say a little more: typically the supply to hair is so liberal that it is estimated that every hair-root is supplied by three separate nerves, springing from the dense nerve-network that lies in the subcutaneous tissue. This implies that each hair-root has a 'three-point bearing' on it, and cartography shows us how accurate this can be in locating a precise position in space. Provided, then, that the hair itself is of a kind that can respond to touch by a deformation of its root (which is where the nerves are, of course) then it can act as an 'antenna' of great receptivity. The difference in receptivity between a long coarse hair (on the head or pubic region) and a short, fine one (on, say, the back of the hand) is

[1] Other titles in the series are given at the beginning of this book, opposite the title page.

obvious enough if one tries the simple experiment of touching them near their tips. Most animals have only the relatively insensitive kind, except for what we know as highly specialized 'whiskers' near the mouth: these are long and relatively thick, but they have a special system of blood-vessels near the roots, which cause them, especially under conditions of excitement, to stand out stiff and quivering. Under these circumstances a touch near the hair-tip is readily transmitted to the root, where the nerve-fibres can pick up the information and convey it to the brain.

The short delicate body hair of man, consisting of nearly two million sensory antennae, represents a major part of the complex sensory system that provides each individual with his link with his environment. We ourselves are products of this same environment. Perhaps the most urgent task that faces us in this century is to see and feel the fact of our union with nature. The idea that man stands outside nature was part of the old romantic delusion of both religion and science. Now that we know it to be false we are faced with great problems as to how to express the insights we have regained about man's links with his fellow-creatures. If you distrust nature, then you will distrust man, and that is what the whole concept of THE NAKED APE does. Alienation is the great disorder of modern man. It is vitally important that scientists and philosophers should demonstrate and illustrate all the links we possess that join us to our environment. The skin, and those tiny, 'puny' hairs that Morris is so scathing about, are vital factors in overcoming the problem of alienation.

THE EVOLUTION OF SENSITIVITY

The evolutionary trend towards exposure of the surface of the skin to the stimuli of the environment has brought enormous positive gains for *Homo sapiens*. Some areas of the body are truly naked, with not a vestige of a hair: apart from the obvious palms and soles of the hands and feet, there is a thin strip of skin immediately adjacent to the lips which has no hair, and also some parts of the genital apparatus in both men and women. Each one of these areas is exquisitely sensitive, with a very complex nerve supply and a big area in the brain given over to the analysis of impulses arising from it. The part of the body with the finest, softest, most delicate hair is the lobe of the ear. This is a feature unique to man, and Morris comments perceptively on its extraordinary sensitivity, especially in response to love play: physical characteristics of the fleshy lobes of the ears can provide pointers to character. The hands and feet with their special 'finger-prints' and their extremely efficient pattern of nerve supply are, of course, extraordinarily sensitive to fine touch. Even though this primary function has been masked in the feet, by the need to provide a firm support for man's upright stance, the soles of the feet are even now more sensitive even than the hands to certain forms of light touch such as tickling. A word might here be said, too, about those much maligned structures, the finger nails. Books on human evolution often seem to dismiss them again as being no more than an evolutionary 'left-over' from the time when we had decent claws on the ends of the digits. Such an interpretation is just another example of that whole reductionist outlook which we challenge in this book. Flat finger-nails are not much good, it is true, for the kind of job that claws do very well. But they are extremely sensitive, as we learn to our cost when we injure them. Because of their very elaborate nerve supply they add to the sensitivity of the finger-tip to an astonishing degree, as is obvious if one has the misfortune to 'lose' a nail in an accident: during the six months or more that it takes to regrow, finger-tip sensitivity is very greatly impaired. Just as with the hair, it is the deformation of the 'root' (nail-bed in this case) that is necessary for the nerve-endings to be able to transmit information, which is what being 'sensitive' is all about. Claws and hooves are adapted for different purposes, and their sensitivity is very much lower. Popular writers may choose to ignore these 'progressive features' (as other trends in other zoological groups would certainly be called) in man, and prefer to dwell on features that look essentially backward to the place of his origin amongst the primates. But then they are missing the most important part by far of the study of human evolution, which is to give some guide, from study of the past, as to the possibilities for the future. The biological trend in the story of *Homo sapiens* is undoubtedly towards increased sensitivity, increased awareness, increased freedom of action. That these features bring great dangers is undeniable. The challenge is enormous. So too is the responsibility. Too many people with power to influence public opinion are only too ready to opt out of their responsibilities in these matters, and to provide excuses for all kinds of regressive and aggressive behaviour patterns. Real science has something much more significant to report.

It is interesting to compare the skin on the two surfaces, front and back, of the forearm. The front is almost 'naked' in the true sense. Here the skin itself is much thinner, and its sensitivity is due in part to the fact that nerve-endings can reach much closer to the surface. Even more sensitive, of course, would be 'raw' nerves—as we discover to our discomfort when an abrasion takes off the superficial layers of skin anywhere, and brings the nerves themselves even closer to the surface. The evolutionary 'problem' for a group like the primates, which has been developing right from its inception on the lines of increased brain-size (and all the things that are necessary before that development can really 'take-off') is how to get the nerves as 'raw' as possible while still providing adequate protection for them in the form of a covering of skin. The front and back of the forearm indicate the balance that has been, or is being, achieved in this regard. The more naturally protected front (the 'flexor-surface' as we call it) has very thin skin, nerve-endings relatively near the surface, and hardly any hair. The back has thicker skin and innumerable hairs whose main 'purpose' in terms of evolutionary tendency is concerned with conveying information about touch-impressions to the nerve-network around the root of the hair-follicle. In this trend, as in so many things, women lead the way. Men with long coarse hair on general body-surfaces are simply not 'advanced' along this path towards 'nakedness'—though of course they may have other very important traits, which make their contribution to the evolutionary process extremely important. Typical feminine gentleness is not always appropriate to biological survival. The typically masculine 'world of doing' is also an essential ingredient of human progress. But if modern psychological analysis is right[1] proper functioning in the 'world of doing' depends on prior participation in the feminine 'world of being'. If such participation is not provided for by the mother or mother-figure in infancy, the chances are that insecurity of personality will result. And it is then, and only then, that the tough, masculine 'world of doing' takes on sinister aspects. Properly developed masculine drives find their natural human outlets in exploration, work, play, and constructive 'doing' of all kinds. It is when the basis has been badly laid that there is the greatest chance that these drives (which of

[1] See the penetrating analysis by David Holbrook: THE DELUSIONS OF SEXOLOGY in *The Cambridge Quarterly* 1968, 3, 234-252.

course are shared in some measure by women too—it is a biological truism that each sex shares the characteristics of the other) will manifest themselves as overt aggression, delinquency and criminal behaviour. It is monstrous that such regrettable aberrations should be counted as evidence that man's real nature is aggressive and cruel. The peculiarities in the evolution of human skin are correlated with increased sensitivity and awareness. If this biological trend is adequately documented and taught it should lead logically to increased co-operative activity, to love and respect amongst human beings. Naked ape or *Homo sapiens*? It is up to us to decide where we want to go, where our history tells us we ought to go.

D

CHAPTER THREE

Is Man a Beast of Prey?

The romance of the Naked Ape and the Greylag Goose has created something of a sensation among the reading public. The authors, Konrad Lorenz and Desmond Morris have suddenly found their books best-sellers, serialised in the press of the English-speaking world, and published in edition after edition in both England and the United States. The reason for this popularity is firstly the entertaining nature of the story—the fascinating picture of fighting fish glowing with irridescent colours as they rush at one another, the love life of the Greylag Goose with the mock heroics of its Triumph Ritual, the fantastic sexual rivalry of baboons, has opened a world of wonder the interest and importance of which no one would wish to deny.

Desmond Morris has written an entertaining book on the parallels between human and anthropoid behaviour based on his experience in the London Zoo. It was here also that he tried to teach a chimpanzee to paint and published an amusing account of it. His original interest in animals was concerned with communication, which in his early years as an artist had greatly interested him. Wishing to investigate how animals communicated he took a University degree in Zoology and then went to the Zoo. His present book is especially concerned with the signals chimpanzees and other anthropoids make to one another and the similarity or contrast between these signals and methods of human communication. The intention being to demonstrate that human behaviour is derived from and largely embodies the behaviour patterns of our ape-like ancestors. If this is so and if "man is certainly an ape", then very significant conclusions follow.

One would have expected Morris to have supported his

arguments from a much wider range of field observations among apes. There is no reference, for instance, to Jane Goodall's interesting work on wild chimpanzees and her special investigations on the mothering instinct in females and the nest-building activities of these apes. She has very ably demonstrated how environmental stresses promote behavioural reorganization—a question which has also been discussed by Le Gros Clark in relation to the rapid development of intelligence in the australopithecines.[1] Nor does Morris seem aware of the work of Adrian Kortlandt, the Dutch chimpanzee expert, in the report of his six African expeditions. These observations, which cover a much wider field than the limited area covered by Morris (which goes little farther than the London Zoo) throw considerable doubt on the similarities he finds between ape and human behaviour.

He is also unlikely to convince either the anthropologists or the psychologists, because he produces evidence for this similarity exclusively from human behaviour patterns in middle-class Britain and the United States, and ignores the rest of the world. Local customs are not universal; far fetched analogies require proof before they can be accepted, and this is not forthcoming.

But of greater importance is the assumption that we may expect to find significant parallels in human and ape behaviour because the apes are our ancestors and the behaviour patterns they display have been established by natural selection. Hence since we manifestly inherit the greater part of our anatomical features and all our physiological processes from our animal ancestors is it not to be expected that we shall inherit those other characteristics which must also have been established genetically—these being the basic instincts, the behaviour patterns, and inherited habits?

This depends of course on narrowing the gap between man and apes, and therefore the argument of THE NAKED APE is concerned first and foremost to demonstrate that, all said and done, man is 'only an animal', and not only an animal but an ape. "Man is certainly an ape!"[2] The whole argument depends on the truth of this statement.

ONLY AN APE?

Morris, therefore, proceeds to develop his argument in order to bridge

[1] Le Gros Clark, W. E. (29).
[2] Montagu, Ivor. Review of THE NAKED APE in *Comment* January 27th, 1968.

the gap between man and the ape; he intends to show that man is only an animal, and not only an animal but an ape: that "Man is certainly ape".

Now by thus equating man with his anthropoid cousins the enormous difference, due to the dawn of reason, the mastery of technology, the discovery of values and the creation of standards of conduct, is pushed into the background. All this can be neglected or reduced to anthropoid behaviour patterns, and the identity with the anthropoids can be proved by showing that human behaviour is 'only' ape behaviour, inherited and modified in this way or that.

The basic pattern of behaviour that we inherit, Morris desires to show, is that of the predatory descendants of the peaceful fruit-eating and tree-dwelling apes who descended to the ground and became hunters. This transition involved radical changes both in the anatomy, the habits, the sexual life, and the behaviour patterns of the new type of animal. These were established by variations which were established by their survival value and passed on by inheritance. Thus our human species entered upon its humanity as "predators whose natural instinct is to kill".[1] We ourselves are determined by them since civilization is so recent that too little time has elapsed to change our biological inheritance.

Unfortunately this theory falls to pieces on various grounds: (1) Man is not descended from the anthropoid apes. The remote ancestors who preceded both man and the modern ape, which takes us back some 35 million years, branched into two divergent lines, one leading to the anthropoid apes or *Pongidae* (chimpanzees, gorillas, orangutans), the other to the *Hominidae*, leading through *Australopithecus* to Man. And since the apes adopted a highly specialized life of their own, both in anatomy and habits, there can be no analogy with the *Hominidae* who developed along totally different lines.

(2) Secondly, hunting does not imply internecine war, aggression, and ferocity. Hunting communities like the Esquimaux are entirely peaceful and co-operative. Peoples living on grain, and hardly eating any meat at all, and there have been plenty of them, have proved just as capable of becoming warlike and predatory as those who live by hunting. This depends not on any hereditary disposition based on how their food is obtained, but on economic and social conditions independent of diversities of diet. Hunting is in fact the most primitive of all econo-

[1] Ardrey, Robert (1), p. 316.

mies, along with simple food gathering of roots and fruits; and in this very early period, up to 40,000 years ago, there is no evidence of war-like behaviour. War reaches the level of the military empires only after the discovery and development of agriculture and the disappearance of hunting as the basis of food getting, a method which would obviously be totally inadequate to feed the great populations of the river valleys of the Middle East, India and China, where, in the Old World, civilization had its origin.

Professor Ashley Montagu, in his book THE DIRECTION OF HUMAN DEVELOPMENT and in a lecture published in the *Los Angeles Times* for May 26th 1968, deals exhaustively with the view that early man is an aggressive killer. On the contrary, he argues, the conditions of man's evolution throughout almost the whole of his two million years of development

"placed a very high premium upon his ability to co-operate. Human populations were very small, of the order of 10 to 100 individuals. In such hunting, food-gathering societies, mutual aid and involvement in the welfare of others were not only highly valued but absolutely indispensable if the group was to survive. . . . Aggressive individuals simply could not flourish in such societies. Hence it is highly improbable that anything remotely resembling an instinct of aggression would have developed, not to mention an instinct for territoriality."[1]

Lorenz repeatedly speaks of the warlikeness of early man. Ashley Montagu refutes this conception, pointing out that

"there is absolutely no evidence of this. Hunting, food-gathering peoples down to this day tend not to be so. There are a few exceptions, but they are rare. Being small in numbers, early man could not have survived long had they made a habit of warfare."[2]

HUMAN AND SUB-HUMAN

This brings us to the basic fallacy which vitiates this whole approach: the attempt to dissipate the fundamental difference between man and

[1] *Los Angeles Times*, May 26th, 1968.
[2] *Ibid.*

the animals. Any argument which ignores the gulf in anatomical structure, intelligence and social organization between ourselves and the anthropoids and is based on comparisons between man and fighting fish, or Greylag geese, or even between man and baboons or chimpanzees, carries no conviction. As Arthur Koestler has pointed out in his review of THE NAKED APE in the *Observer*, the zoological portrait of man thus presented is not only an over-simplification but

"to leave out of account technology and verbalization—that is to say, language, science and art, the essential trademarks of our species—leads inevitably not only to a simplified but to a distorted picture, because these activities permeate and transform even those aspects of behaviour which we share with other species, such as feeding, fighting, mating and care of the young."

We live in quite another world from the apes. Stereotyped behaviour patterns, apart from those we create for ourselves, are not characteristic of man. We *learn* to make appropriate responses to new and intricate situations, where significant features are by no means as obvious as those which the chimpanzee grasps when he engages in sexual play or rakes bananas into his cage. Man is infinitely malleable. He is not organically specialized in the sense of having his reactions determined by a set of instinctual drives. The mind and behaviour of man, as we propose to show, operates on an entirely different level.

It is necessary at this point to turn to the theories of Freud, since all three ethologists seek to buttress their theories of man's inherited behaviour patterns with the Freudian conception of the instinctual basis of human conduct. No one would wish to deny the very great contribution of Freud to contemporary thinking. There are psycho-analytic insights into the motives and mechanisms of men that are of the first importance not only to the educator and psychologist but equally to the doctor and the social scientist. But the Freudian cosmology presents a confused picture of mythological and rational elements; and the mythology least capable of rational justification is the attribution of every phase of man's social existence to some inner urge, as if civilization were one pure reflection and objective elaboration of 'human nature', and assuming a whole series of explanatory instincts as primary and culture as wholly derivative from them.

Freud reduces these instincts to an undifferentiated energy capable of infinite variation. This is his *libido* theory which postulates a force which is mainly sexual, a biological drive rooted in the body with its unalterable hereditary constitution. This is not far from Hobbes' view of human nature, which depicts society as a mass of isolated individuals whose natural emotion is hostility, pushing and jostling each other in the name of survival of the fittest, but willing under certain circumstances to band together to resist external aggression or to secure under due laws of war a temporary armistice to prevent mutual destruction, as hedgehogs might cluster together for warmth.

Freud sees civilization as a repressive force holding down this *libido* (or the *id*) by the authority of the implanted super-ego—the irrational conscience introjected into the mind by the combined pressure of parents and society.

"Civilization, suppression and neurosis are inevitably associated in such a way that the more civilization, the more neurosis—the less suppression, the less neurosis and the less civilization."[1]

Man is not a rational animal but a repressed animal. And the conflict cannot be resolved. We shall never "dislodge the greatest obstacle to civilization, the constitutional tendency in men to aggression."[2] The hatred we repress with difficulty remains the mainspring of our social life.

Thus Freud has elected to regard *aggressiveness*, and delight in inflicting pain on others, as a primary quality, and self-humiliation and delight in suffering hurt from others as a revulsion from this. Whatever form of human organization we consider, he argues, from the family to the nation, or the nation to a world community, the fundamental aggressiveness in man which desires the death of others (and in the last analysis of himself)[3] will threaten and may in the long run break it.

Freud's theory, like all attempts to explain human conduct by hypostasising an innate instinct or drive for each tendency, whether

---

[1] Brown, J. A. C. (11), p. 113.
[2] Freud, S. (18), pp. 138, 139.
[3] Freud developed his original theory of the aggressive drive into the notion of what was primarily self-destructive (*Thanatos* the death wish), an endeavour to return to the original, inorganic state of complete freedom from tension or striving—Nirvana. Freud regarded external aggression (and also sexual sadism) as a safety valve for an impulse which would otherwise prove entirely self-destructive. *He advances no new evidence for this theory.* It is for him dependent for its truth solely on his powerfully subjective conviction!

that is ultimately part of man's essential nature (Freud) or genetically transmitted from our animal ancestors (Lorenz, Ardrey, Morris), is open to the objection that it substitutes a metaphysical entity for an ascertainable and *testable* cause.

Freud's theory cannot be tested because it is so constructed as to be immune from refutation by negative instances. Where there is no evidence for aggressive tendencies, Freud attributes this to exceptionally powerful and successful repression which indicates the damming up of aggressive emotion. Thus, as Popper points out[1], we have here a theory which is constructed so as to be compatible with any kind of evidence: both with that which justifies the existence of the instinctive cause for aggression and that which contradicts it. Yet Lorenz, Ardrey and Morris all justify their theories of an innate drive to aggression by appealing to Freud.

Freud's theories are generally accepted as supporting the view that war is the inevitable result of man's inherent instinct of aggression.[2] In fact he goes so far as to say that if this aggression is *not* directed outwards in war, it would destroy the nation with internal feuds—a view very like that of Robert Ardrey, who argued that internal peace was only secured by the release of aggression against the forces of enmity arrayed against us; and also Russell's, who argued that it was only "the external enemy which supplied the cohesive force of society", so that "A world state, if it were firmly established, would have no enemies to fear, and would therefore be in danger of breaking down through lack of cohesive force."[3]

ON TAKING 'AGGRESSION' SERIOUSLY

One sometimes hears it said that Lorenz and the others are not personally aggressive or reactionary persons and certainly have no intention of promoting war. No-one would accuse them of this for a moment, but perhaps for that very reason their theories will gain an acceptance which they never would if they were advanced by those who might be regarded as 'war mongers'. It is however often said that by 'aggression' they don't really mean aggression at all. Anthony Storr

[1] Popper, K. (42) and (43).
[2] Glover, E. (20).
[3] Russell, Bertrand (44), p. 19.

says that he only means the harmless but necessary drive to overcome obstacles and strive persistently to obtain our goals (though elsewhere he regards it as the basic cause of war). Ivor Montagu[1] argues that 'aggression' in the language of animal behaviour has nothing to do with aggression in the language of statecraft and how to prevent war. It is sometimes purely symbolical—including singing or displaying bright colours at one another. 'Aggression' in ethology, we are told, has no pejorative sense whatever. Often it does not even mean violence and it rarely means damage.

This reminds one of Freud's 'erotic impulse' which comes to mean anything and everything that has a directive or hormic significance in human life, everything that provides a motive, creates an urge or reflects a value. So 'aggression' now comes to mean really whatever you like. But this is an unsatisfactory procedure, for *anything may be maintained if one takes the liberty of using words now in a broader and again in a narrower sense, first comprehensively; and then in a highly specific sense.*

The danger, in the case of the word 'aggression', especially when it is used by a liberal minded person, is that he always insists that it is perfectly innocuous and so, largely on his own reputation as a peaceably minded man, can get the *principle* of an '*aggressive instinct*' widely accepted. But those who are now convinced that man is innately aggressive find that the writers who established the principle (the Lorenzs, the Ardreys, the Russells, the Freuds, and Desmond Morris himself) do themselves in fact regard the principle as demonstrating the inevitability of war, indeed its *utility*, its necessity, and so indeed does Anthony Storr.

The liberal defenders of 'aggression' thus become a kind of decoy to lure us into the more intransigent position and to gain wide acceptance for a principle which once it is conceded leads inevitably to conclusions which they themselves both deplore and accept.

Ardrey declares that man inevitably *invades* adjacent nations. He speaks of constantly probing others' 'territory', for "we are predators", and, as we have seen, makes internal peace dependent on "combating the external enemy". War is necessary, he says, if society is to hold together. Lorenz argues that "the *destructive intensity* (our italics) of the aggression drive, still a hereditary evil of mankind, is the consequence of a process of intra-specific selection which worked

[1] Ivor Montagu, *Marxism Today*, April 1968.

on our forefathers for roughly 40,000 years."[1] And although in the
course of evolution it has been 'redirected', that only means that it is
turned away from the species to the outside enemy. Without this
antagonism, and the corresponding aggression against others, the
social bond within cannot develop. The lethal character of this
aggression was at first however limited because the weaker could and
did make gestures of submission; but now distance, when we kill with
a rifle, does not allow us to receive submissive signals[2] from our
enemies, and war has become far more dangerous. We even suffer
today, he continues, from "insufficient discharge of the aggressive
drive"[3]. Thus when peace was imposed on certain Indian tribes they
suffered from neurosis; and that may be our trouble if war is abolished.
Peace can become a serious menace!

Desmond Morris is quite clear as to the implications of his
view of human nature. He declares that when optimism is expressed
as to our ability to re-mould our way of life, "control our aggressive
and territorial feelings", and "dominate all our basic urges, I submit
that this is rubbish. Our raw animal nature will never permit this."[4]

Anthony Storr can see very little chance of reducing hostility.
"No mutation has occurred to render us radically different
from our prehistoric ancestors: and we possess the same
instinctive equipment which served to ensure the survival of
men for whom existence was a perpetual struggle."[5]

Ivor Montagu declares that
"The inborn restraints that have sufficed to enable the
species to survive despite its dangerous potential are not
adapted to operate effectively against man's present
increased destructive potential."[6]

MAN AS A BEAST OF PREY

What is fundamental to this position is the identification of man with
the sub-human: 'Not only an animal but an ape', 'certainly an ape',
'the only carnivore among apes', 'killers armed with lethal weapons',

[1] Lorenz, Konrad (31), p. 34.
[2] *Op. cit.* pp. 207-208.
[3] *Op. cit.* p. 209.
[4] Morris, Desmond (36), p. 241.
[5] Storr, Anthony (51), p. 111.
[6] Ivor Montagu, *Comment*, January 27th, 1968.

'a predator whose natural instinct is to kill'—in other words man is essentially 'a beast of prey'. As Oswald Spengler, the German philosopher who contributed powerfully to the ideology of the Nazi movement, declared in 1931:

"The beast of prey is the highest form of active life. It represents a mode of living which demands the extreme degree of the necessity of fighting, conquering, annihilating self-assertion. The human race ranks highly because it belongs to the class of beasts of prey. Therefore we find in man the tactics of life proper to a bold, cunning beast of prey. He lives engaged in aggression, killing, annihilation. He wants to be master in as much as he exists"

said Spengler in 1931[1]. He never abandoned this view; in his last book he returns to the theme.

"Man is a beast of prey. I shall say it again and again. The traders in virtue, the champions of social ethics, are but beasts of prey with their teeth broken."[2]

If this is indeed the situation, can we deal with it only by moral exhortation, sermons, education? Can you preach vegetarianism to tigers? Is not the result likely to be that despair at 'the human condition' which is the dominant note of our times? The preacher of morals in such a world as ours is liable to an overwhelming feeling of futility, ineffectiveness, for the belief that eloquence and passionate exhortation must in the end prevail inevitably results in disillusionment and despair.

But if we can understand that aggression is not due to an ineradicable instinct, but, as psychologists have explained, is due to resentment at injustice, is the protest of the under-privileged, the cry of the oppressed creature; or, when it appears in the young, can be the result of faults in upbringing, to parental and adult repression—could we not see the possibility of preventing it by dealing with its underlying causes and so lessen the likelihood both of interpersonal and international conflict?

DOES 'INSTINCT' EXPLAIN?

The attempt to explain human behaviour, especially in the more

1 Spengler, Oswald (49).
2 Spengler, Oswald (50).

reprehensible forms, as due to our animal instincts, breaks down on three counts:

(1) Why should we regard hunting as a method of obtaining food as necessarily implying aggression to one's fellows? It is no more a vicious proceeding in itself than our going for lamb chops or fishing for trout. It is in no way correlated with social strife. Lorenz points out that even carnivores when hunting are not *angry*, as they can be when fighting for their lives, and man is not even a carnivore. Social violence is no more prevalent among carnivores than among herbivorous animals. Lorenz admits that entirely peaceful animals will fight when harassed and cornered; so they will if reduced to completely abnormal conditions by overcrowding. Is this evidence for a dangerous urge to violence? One is reminded of the famous remark: "This animal is extremely ferocious. It defends itself when attacked."

Animals are not ferocious just because they are animals. We do them an injustice by blaming them for our crimes. Most animals live very peaceably together, and intra-specific aggression is rare except under abnormal conditions of over-crowding. Carnivores act as predators when requiring food, but this does not mean that they are continuously angry, irrascible, quarrelsome and dangerous. In their domestic lives, and in relation to the animals they do not feed on, carnivores are as without malice as other animals. And, moreover, man is not a carnivore. His dentition lacks the powerful canine teeth present in all beasts of prey and present even in the apes.

There is nothing like the permanent instinct to invade, to destroy, to attack other members of the species, attributed to man, in any animal; as far as the herbivorous and omnivorous animals, to which group we belong and from which we have descended, are concerned, they are even less disposed to any kind of ferocity, and the apes were peaceful fruit eaters.

(2) Secondly the basic neurological and psychological difference from the animals is the fact that man is not a system of built-in mechanical reaction patterns—like fish, reptiles and birds, and to a less extent mammals. The insect's behaviour is almost completely instinctual and unalterable. Other animals too show behaviour largely constituted by conditioned reflexes and instincts. Not so man, whose nature is the results of the interaction of biological and social inheritances, and is for that reason variable and mutable. Basic are the biological *needs* for food, shelter, warmth and the like, which are not fixed instinctive

reactions, but *needs* which find all sorts of different ways to satisfying themselves, whereas an instinct is, by definition, a fixed response to the same stimulus.

Man has a minimum of instincts of this kind. He has all the basic needs which he fulfils by means of his elaborate technological methods in agriculture and industry; and he has superimposed his own civilized needs for culture and recreation on these. It is therefore quite mistaken to explain man in terms of the built-in reactions of animals lacking in the capacity to plan their actions on the bases of elaborate roundabout methods and tools requiring intelligence, foresight, imagination and planning. An animal has none of these capacities. He lives entirely in the present, as all animal psychology insists. (3) Finally to account for anything, and especially human behaviour, by invoking an 'instinct' for every kind of conduct we want to explain, is pure superstition and fundamentally unscientific. It reminds one of the character in Molière's play who explained the power of opium to send one to sleep by 'the soporific principle' which it contained.

This resort to some 'instinct' or 'principle' as an explanation really tells us nothing: Man's behaviour is determined by his instincts, we are told: If he goes with his fellows it is the 'herd instinct' which actuates him; if he walks alone, it is the 'anti-social instinct'; if he fights, it is the instinct of 'pugnacity' or 'aggression'; if he is of a peaceful disposition or gives in, it is the instinct of 'self-abasement'; if he twiddles his thumbs, it is the 'thumb-twiddling' instinct; thus everything is very satisfactorily explained. But have we got an inch further?

Modern psychology does not proceed by such means. It seeks for the particular conditions which can be shown to be responsible for fear, or anger, or aggression, in the absence of which the phenomenon does not appear. This is the only valid kind of scientific explanation. Merely to invoke a principle, or invent some plausible myth, is insufficient because the 'principle' says nothing at all, but merely gives a name to the problem, while a myth, or story, or theory which simply accounts for the fact in a plausible way, does not exclude a dozen other plausible theories, and we are left with a welter of contradictory views none of which can be proved or disproved.

We come back to the necessity for *testing* an hypothesis if it is to be acceptable. Plausibility is never enough. In every case we must demand some method of distinguishing a true explanatory theory from a false one or an inadequate one, and this cannot depend on its plausibility. Plausible to whom? This is surely wholly relative to our feelings; and if men, as they certainly do, have very different opinions as to what *seems* to them true, we are left entirely in the air. This is why we can only proceed in scientific argument with hypotheses which are susceptible to experimental proof or disproof.

INSTINCT OR INTELLIGENCE?

Contrary to the speculations of Ardrey and Lorenz, when, in the course of his evolution, man took to hunting, the highest premium was placed on co-operation and adaptability. The more primitive type of fixed instinctive reaction, modified by trial-and-error learning, would have served no useful function. On the contrary such fixed patterns of reaction would have been in the way.

"Learning to make one's way in the human environment, the man-made environment, was what was required, not biologically determined reactions to situations for which they were neither designed nor appropriate, but thought out solutions to the novel and continually changing challenges of the environment."[1]

The outstanding characteristic of man is his capacity for this kind of response to the demands of the environment. The kind of response found in other creatures keeps them fixed in their ecological niches and simply would not work in the ever changing situations in which man finds himself. Other animals adapt themselves to their environment by responses which are genetically more limited and more fixed.

"So far as his psychological responses to the world are concerned man is almost wholly emancipated from dependence upon inherited biological dispositions, uniquely improving upon the latter by his ability to learn that which his social heredity, his culture, makes available to him."[2]

It is a very common assumption, encouraged by such popularizations of early man as we find in the books under discussion, that man originated as an aggressive, hostile, belligerent cannibal, killing dinosaurs with his stone axe and dragging his women folk about by

[1] Montagu, Ashley, *Los Angeles Times*, May 26th, 1968.
[2] Montagu, Ashley (35), p. 46.

the hair. This view has, of course, received considerable support from the views often attributed to Freud. Dr. M. E. Harding, a psychiatrist of the Jungian school provides a typical example of this.[1]

> "Beneath the decent facade of consciousness with its disciplined moral order and good intentions, lurk the crude instinctive forces of life, like monsters of the deep—devouring, begetting, warring endlessly."

This tradition is a myth, but many of us believe in it as if it were a universally established truth. Hence the further myth of our social evolution from bestial, savage, prehistoric ancestors who were in a continuous state of warfare. Contrary to this view the evidence indicates that prehistoric man was, on the whole, a more peaceful, co-operative, unwarlike, unaggressive creature than we are, and that we of the civilized world have in historical time become more aggressive in many ways.

The more modern psychological approach to aggression does not proceed on the assumption that we are dealing with an inborn propensity. What it seeks to do for the person whose basic drives have been frustrated and disordered, and whose neurosis is an expression of that disorder, is to relieve him of the factors of deformation and frustration, and to restore to him the ability to face life in a normal way.

Modern psychology has been extraordinarily successful in discovering the precise situations of frustration or inferiority or fear which lead to aggression on the one hand and withdrawal symptoms on the other. As Karen Horney has shown, it is a neurosis which arises when

> 'the environment is dreaded as a whole, and is felt to be unreliable, mendacious, unappreciative, unfair, unjust, greedy and a menace to the entire development of the individual."[2]

So far we have only dealt with the ethologists on the basis of their own rather confused arguments and the support they have found for their theories in Freud. What we have now to do is to turn to the theory of evolution and see whether that theory ever really identifies man with the apes, or whether it does not reveal a sharp break, which establishes what Julian Huxley calls *The Uniqueness of Man*.

[1] Harding, M. E. (21), p. 1.
[2] Horney, Karen (22) quoted in Brown, J. A. C. (11), p. 137.

We can then proceed to investigate the *psychological* differences—what Teilhard calls 'the leap from zero to infinity'—which establish not only man's capacity for reasoning, but start man off on the course of a *new kind of evolution* which is not biological, and established by inherited physical variations, but social, technological and cultural, the phase in which man makes himself, and changes himself, by developing civilization through its successive stages. If we can come to understand this we shall realize that in man Nature did not merely create a naked ape but transcended herself, that man is not merely an animal repeated, but something more and something better.

CHAPTER FOUR

Man and Evolution

It appears to be assumed by those who consider that man is "only an animal", and derives his basic instincts from his ancestors, that if man has really evolved from the higher primates, he cannot essentially be anything else.[1]

But evolutionary processes can never be evaluated or even adequately described in terms of their origin. They must be defined by their *direction*, their achieved *differences*, their inherent possibilities, and their deducible *future trends*.

Generic continuity—yes; but also striking differences. In evolution the *difference* is as essential as the *continuity*. It is defined as 'descent with change': it is not mere descent. As Sellars says, we are confronted with pluses. Biological properties are not the same as chemical, psychological are not identical with biological.

"Growth implies both identity and difference. The higher levels cannot be led back to the lower without a remainder . . . It is not that any new entity has made its appearance, but that the system has become more complex and more highly organized. It is the organization which is novel and with which new properties must be correlated."[2]

Continuity of the new with the old does not mean, therefore, that in the new we find 'nothing but' its origins. What something

---

[1] Except perhaps in a quantitative way; that is to say he may have *more* intelligence, and perhaps other characteristics too may be more marked in man than in his ancestors.

[2] Sellars, R. W. (46), pp. 331-337.

develops *from* does not necessarily determine and limit the nature of that thing. Mammals evolved from reptiles, and reptiles from amphibians, and amphibians from fish. But a mammal is *not* some kind of amphibian though it evolved from one. Its warm blood, its hairy skin, the development of the young within the mother, and a host of other defining characteristics assert the *difference* from the amphibian, and still more from the fish. A chick develops from an egg. Is the chick then only a peculiar kind of egg?

Why then, if man developed from an ape, or a primate who was the ancestor of both apes and men, is "man certainly an ape"? There is no more reason to call him an ape than to call him a frog or a fish. That he shares more characteristics with the ape, is not a convincing reason. The mammal shares an immense range of organic and biological processes with the fish. The question remains, *is there something really new*? If so, the philosophy of 'nothing but' does not hold.

THE SUCCESSION OF INTEGRATIVE LEVELS

Evolution sees the history of this planet as a continuous development, uninterrupted by supernatural interventions, whereby *inorganic matter* first produces a new level of reality, *life*;[1] and life, evolving from simple organisms to immensely complex ones, passes through a series of rising levels, to produce the highest level yet reached, thinking man.

These successive phases are best known as *integrative levels*,[2] because what makes the difference is a greater *complexity* of pattern. The essence of the process is that, first, there exist things with a determinate structure and character of their own, and then, that these things arrange themselves into a new pattern, which as a whole possesses a new type of structure and a new order of qualities. The fundamental conception here implied is the conception that quality depends on *pattern*.[3]

The emergent qualities and processes at each level are the characteristics and laws of this higher form of organization, which are

[1] This development has been admirably expounded in Bernal, J. D. (7).
[2] Needham, Joseph (37).
[3] Thus if you arrange the atoms of Copper, Sulphur and Oxygen in a particular pattern it gives you a blue crystal known as *copper sulphate*, which has totally different properties from its constituents.

found only at this level of complexity. Of course, the more complex quality includes in itself elements of the simpler—there is no organic life without its constituent physico-chemical processes—but the elements of the old, by being subordinated to the new system, by entering into the new synthesis, themselves become something new. Within the organism, that is the living thing, they undergo a radical change; they cease to be limited by the reactions covered by existing laws.

Thus the unique condition of the *chemical* processes within an *organism* are such that they reach results that under *inorganic* conditions are impossible. The new properties and laws then belong to the newly organized whole, and to it alone. It is a *qualitatively unique* form of structure and movement, which, since it proceeds from previous stages of the development, includes in itself elements of the old and re-fashions them in a new system.

(a) Very largely the living organism can build up the complex proteins of its living cells out of simpler organic substances; or, as in plants, out of purely inorganic material.

(b) It can produce independent organisms similar to itself.

(c) It is not merely acted upon by its environment. It becomes aware of it, and reacts selectively to its own advantage—and so on.

The important thing to note is that what appears is *wholly new*, and must not be denied existence by being reduced to 'nothing but' the elements and processes on which it depends, as though one were to deny the existence of a cathedral as a cathedral because it was '*made of*' nothing but stones, or of a symphony, the beauty of which depends on the harmonies, sequences and modulations of the notes, as though it were *only* vibrations of different rates.

But on the other hand the insistence on the *reality*, the novelty, the qualitative emergence of the unpredictable, does not imply the addition *from without* of 'life', or 'beauty' or whatever unexpected quality has appeared. Thus we have developmental *continuity*, without the injection of the new from some transcendental source, united with the *emergence* of most striking differences. Evolution may therefore be described as the active rise of the new wholes with new properties.

If the leap to the level of the organic, of living matter, is surprising, still more so is the emergence of 'mind'. One of the characteristics of life, as we have seen, is 'irritability', the power to respond selectively to the environment, to be aware of it, to seek some elements in it and reject others. We do not call this *mind* at this early stage; but 'irritability', or sensitivity, itself develops through a series of stages, each qualitatively new in its turn, until in the large-brained mammal, we have a most extraordinary capacity for responding to the environmental stimuli and adjusting itself to the external world. What happens when we come to man? The psychologist is in no doubt at all. He asserts a function of reason absent in the lower mammals.[1] Here again the qualitative emergence is undeniable unless one is under the constraint of a metaphysical dogma which insists that evolution means continuity in the sense of identity, and excludes the emergence of the wholly new and unpredictable.

Does the appearance of this new quality require a special creation, the *insertion* of 'mind' into the animal body by some supernatural agency? Not at all. It is only the 'nothing but' thinker who would be compelled to that explanation, if he at last saw the absurdity of reducing mental activities, thinking, to 'nothing but' physical reactions, movements of the lips and throat, as the Behaviourists do. The emergent evolutionist sees it as a further stage in a world process that *in itself* is capable of moving from level to level. Just as life emerged from the inorganic, so 'thinking' becomes a characteristic of living organisms with highly developed nervous systems.

If mind is thought of as a *function* of the brain, and not as a 'thinking substance' added to the body to interact with it, as Descartes supposed, we avoid the baffling problem he left us with as to how 'pure thought' could control 'solid matter'. We are no longer baffled by the mystery of 'the ghost in the machine'.[2]

Regarding thinking as a function of brains and as dependent upon them does not mean that we *reduce* it to physicochemical processes, that is to 'nothing but' the physiological events without which it would not occur. We reject the outdated materialism which describes mind as 'only' chemical processes—or as an *epiphenomenon*, a byproduct, which exerts no appreciable influence on the subsequent development of the process, like the mark made by chalk on a blackboard, or the red glow of a heated iron bar. It has its own undeniable qualitative reality and effectiveness.

[1] See Chapter 6, 'The Explosion of Mind'.
[2] Ryle, Gilbert (45), p. 16.

We do not say that life is *only* chemistry; and we do not say that mind is *only* the activity of cortical neurones; just as we do not say that man is *only* an ape. We recognize the emergence of the entirely new.

We have a puerile conception of evolution if it is without leaps. A genuine conception of evolution, answering actual reality, must embrace not only gradual changes, but also sudden changes, leaps, breaks in continuity. Without such leaps no phenomenon can be explained, for it would be necessary to assume that nothing new can arise, and that everything already exists that will eventually appear.

A very interesting example of the consequence of failing to recognize the fact of emergence, of novelty, is to be found in the opposite direction; this is the theory of *preformation* which held that whatever turns up must have been there to start with, like the duck that 'emerges' from the pond but was really there all the time, but out of sight beneath the surface, or as the tune you get the Juke Box to play was already there and only needed the right stimulus, sixpence in the slot, for it to emerge. Thus biologists once believed that in the spermatozoon was a tiny man, quite complete, the *homunculus*, who grew bigger and bigger when planted in the uterus. This curious conception follows the failure to recognize the *differences* that occur in the course of development. There is no *man*, there is no kind of multicellular organism, in a spermatazoon or a fertilized ovum. It is no more than a single cell, without organs and consciousness. Are we to say that the developed embryo is nothing but what it developed from, or are we to say that since this is absurd it must have contained the homunculus? Or are we to accept the theory of the emergence of the new, by stages, as the product of the sequence of integrative levels?

We must say, therefore, that mind is a new quality or level of existence in the order of evolution, which comes into being with living bodies possessing a complex nervous system. As the Aristotelian puts it, we must not think of 'a mind' as an entity attaching itself to the body, but rather, using the verb rather than the noun, of '*minding*' —the process which goes on when a living body, with its brain, is actually exercising its proper functions. *What seeing is to the eye*, Aristotle might have said, *that the mind is to the organism as a whole*. At the lowest level in simple animals it still represents something unique—we call it 'behaviour'. It is a matter of *response* and not merely the suffering of an external impact. When we study the behaviour of any animal, although we are aware of the dependence on brain, sense organs and motor reactions, we study the living creature as a whole in its world.

At this level behaviour, while representing a form of awareness, does not imply self-consciousness in the human sense. But we now proceed from animals to human behaviour, to the level of rational intelligence. This includes all the automatisms and habits, acquired or innate, which consciousness presupposes, and also the more automatic and conditioned response of the lower levels, but in addition the power of abstract thought.

We perceive then that the evolution of living organisms is more than the continuous modification of form to adjust the organism more closely to its environment. It is also an evolution of *behaviour*. Beginning with the simple response of the protozoon, it reaches a new level with the central control of even a lowly brain, and a surprisingly higher level in the insect with its elaborate instincts. In the mammal we have less instinct and the beginning of intelligence, and in man the dawn of reason.

This process with its successive emergent levels has been well described by Teilhard de Chardin.

"Life is the rise of consciousness . . . Here and there, at the base of nervous systems, psychic tension is doubtless increasing . . . In the higher insects a cephalic concentration of nerve ganglions goes hand in hand with an extraordinary wealth and precision of behaviour . . ."

Yes, but then progress is arrested. They become stationary. They show a strange psychic inferiority. Their psychology has become mechanised and hardened. But among the vertebrates things are still moving, and when we observe the mammals, this

"furry quadruped seems so 'animated' compared with an ant, so genuinely alive . . . There is such suppleness, such unexpectedness, such exuberance of life and curiosity! Instinct is no longer narrowly canalised, as in the spider and the bee, paralysed to a single function. Individually and socially it remains flexible . . . Around it an 'aura' of freedom begins to float, a glimmer of personality. And it is in that direction that the possibilities presently crop up, interminate and interminable, before it."[1]

[1] Teilhard de Chardin, P. (52), pp. 153-155.

THE UNITY OF THE CONSCIOUS ORGANISM

Whatever the organism now is—electronic, atomic, molecular, cellular, subconscious, conscious—it is in each one of these respects also an organization. At each level there is a quality not present at any lower level, something qualitatively new, of a different order from the preceding lower levels, and at that level the organism acts as a unit. Cells are qualitatively different from their contents, and act as units in relation to other cells. And so we proceed up to the whole animal, and ultimately to man. The organism is the organization of the sub-systems, its organs. It is not a *collection* of these. It is the organization of all of them. And it is a hierarchy. The higher rules the lower levels. There is something which transcends all the parts that go to make up the animal itself; and this entity is not only *one*, but is *different* from these parts.

How then do we clearly establish the fundamental *difference* and superiority of man from the animals more convincingly than by establishing the uniqueness of his mind—and as has wisely been said, the importance of this is as necessary for the sake of the ethics of life as for pure knowledge. The dawn of reason and with it self-consciousness marks an immense transformation, visible as clearly in nature as any of the facts recorded by physics or astronomy. Another world is born. Abstraction, logic, reasoned choice and invention, mathematics, art, calculation of space and time, anxieties and dreams of love—all these activities of *inner life*, witness to the vast change that has taken place.

EVOLUTIONARY PROGRESS

And now let us look back at this whole sequence of events in time to ask ourselves two questions: does this series of integrative levels indicate progress, can we see within it a *direction*? No biologist or psychologist would question for a moment a steady movement to qualitatively higher evolutionary levels, the fact that this succession of breaks or leaps reveal to us qualities which are not only *new*, but *higher*.

Secondly, are we to explain this by the interference with the natural order by some external force, or are we to see the natural order itself as capable of giving birth to novelty, as in a sense stepping upward? Here again the natural scientist does not find himself compelled to hold reality to one level, to the lowest, which would be to deny his own empirical data. He must therefore see the world as a self-operating, self-transforming process, he must and does accept the fact that nature transcends itself in the evolutionary process by constantly rising higher than its source.

Any denial of this can only be in the interests of *a priori* metaphysics which is determined in spite of the facts to hold things at one level and refuse the possibility of change and progress. But it is the business of philosophy not to dictate to the facts, not to tell us what it will allow to happen, but to interpret the facts in all their complexity and objectivity. Things are what they are, and we are not permitted to explain them away.

It is only in the face of a reductionist metaphysics, an out-of-date philosophy of monistic materialism, that this can be done. Contemporary philosophy accepts *process and change* as essential characteristics of the natural order—not as something to be inserted from outside, or denied because that kind of explanation is ruled out. It cannot be ruled out without denying the fact that nature is essentially process and activity—a view which makes no concessions to animism or vitalism, or any confusion between the vital process in an organism, the function of mind in man, the physical process in an atom.

This is admirably put by Teilhard de Chardin[1]

"Those who adopt the spiritual explanation are right when they defend so vehemently a certain transcendence of man over the rest of nature. But neither are the materialists wrong when they maintain that man is just one further term in a series of animal forms. Here, as in so many cases, the two antithetical kinds of evidences are resolved in a movement—provided that, however, in this movement the essential part is allowed to the highly natural phenomenon of the 'change of state'. From the cell to the thinking animal, as from the atom to the cell, a single process . . . goes on without interruption and always in the same direction. But by virtue of this permanence in the operation, it is inevitable from the point of view of physics that certain

[1] Teilhard de Chardin, P. (52), p. 169.

leaps suddenly transform the subject of the operation."[1]

Julian Huxley finds this extraordinary process one of evolutionary development *upwards*, in spite of regression here and there (in parasites), and paralysis, stability, in other types. He is not saying by any means that *all* forms progress; or that all of them continuously progress, but that progress *has* taken place and *is* taking place.

Evolutionary progress can be defined as improvement of vital organization permitting increase in control over the environment and in independence of changes in the environment, together with the capacity to continue evolution further in the same general progressive direction.[2]

Huxley advances two criteria of progress:

1   Increasing independence of or control over the environment.

2   The potentiality for further progress.

The mammals including man have fulfilled the first condition. But man has proceeded to a control over and modification of the environment quite beyond the capabilities of the sub-human world. Instead of the endless repetition of a built-in mechanism, we search out more effective ways of suiting the means to the end, we build our own mechanisms, and improve them, and replace them with better ones.

And further, in man reason takes the place of instinct. "What distinguishes the most incompetent architect from the best of bees," Marx once said, "is that the architect raises his structure in imagination before he constructs it in reality." Man realizes his own purposes in external nature by controlling and manipulating it. Premeditated, planned action directed towards definite ends known in advance is the unique characteristic of the human species. Because of this the character of the change effected in the environment is quite different from and more extensive than that effected by any animal. The animal merely *uses* external nature, man changes it to make it serve his ends, *masters* it. Man is the only one amongst the animals capable of creating his own conditions of life, capable of making his own history. The history of animals is made for them, their normal condition is given by the conditions in which they live and to which they adapt themselves.

---

1 Teilhard adds as a footnote the statement that there is nothing to prevent the thinker who adopts a spiritual explanation from positing under the phenomenal veil of a revolutionary transformation, whatever creative operation he likes. But this does not require that, considered as phenomenon, the sequence of levels in developing nature require anything beyond what empirical investigation discovers.

2 Huxley, J. S. (24), pp. 562 and 564.

Man alone is capable of making his own history, and in doing so, making and remaking his patterns of behaviour, himself.

Huxley declares that only in one direction is evolutionary progress now proceeding. Apart from minor adaptations to the environment, evolution has slowed down, and as far as the class of mammals is concerned has reached its end, *with the exception of man*, who alone shows the potentiality for further progress.

Man alone, he says, "continues evolution farther in the same general progressive direction"; and he can do this because of his own evolutionary leap which takes him out of the sub-human animal world. Man is not 'only an ape'; he is not 'only an animal'. He is a mammal, but not only a mammal. His physical organism in certain vital respects shows a definite advance, but these anatomical differences are the basis for the appearance of abstract reason, a new level of intelligence, which starts man on a new career not of bodily changes but of psycho-social evolution, to use Huxley's phrase—that is to say the creation of a civilization and its development. It is on this plane that evolution now continues, in the development of civilization and the recreation at every step forward of man himself.

It is to the uniqueness of man therefore that we now direct our attention.

The following books, not referred to in the text, may also be consulted:

Barnett, A., THE HUMAN SPECIES, A BIOLOGY OF MAN (1957). MacGibbon and Kee, and Penguin.

Bergson, H., CREATIVE EVOLUTION (1911). Macmillan.

De Beer, Gavin, A HANDBOOK ON EVOLUTION (British Museum of Natural History) (1958)

Carrington, R., A MILLION YEARS OF MAN (1963). Weidenfeld and Nicolson.

Collingwood, R. G., THE IDEA OF NATURE (1945). Clarendon Press, Oxford.

Cornwall, I. W., THE MAKING OF MAN (Illustrated account of Primate development and fossil man) (1966). Phoenix House, London.

Lewis, J., MAN AND EVOLUTION (1962). Lawrence & Wishart, London.

Simpson, G. G., THE MEANING OF EVOLUTION (1950). Oxford University Press.

CHAPTER FIVE

The Uniqueness of Man

The very common idea that man is descended from some ape-like ancestor comparable to the Anthropoid apes we know so well—the Chimpanzee, the Gorilla and the Orangutan—is entirely without foundation. This group of animals is known as the *Pongidae*, while the group to which early man belongs is called the *Hominidae*. The latter are not descended from the Pongidae, which is pretty obvious since they are our contemporaries. Who then were the ancestors of the primitive men? There are two theories: (1) About 35,000,000 years ago there lived in Egypt some ape-like creatures, of which *one* fossil— part of a skull—has been found. This animal, a possible precursor of the ancestors of modern man, has been called *Propliopithecus*. It has been thought that from this group, or a group in many ways like it, the primate line evolved to the *Hominidae*, to man.

This fossil is represented by the lower jaw of a small monkey or ape-like creature. This is quite unlike the jaw of the possible ancestors of the apes, probably represented by another Egyptian fossil, of roughly the same period, called *Aegyptopithecus*, the jaw of which is similar to the ape-like jaws and teeth of *Proconsul* and the higher apes, with well marked canines. Is it round about this time that the great divergence of the lines leading to man on the one hand and the apes on the other took place?[1]

(2) Some 19,000,000 years ago there lived in East Africa a different type of ape well on the way to the Pongidae, but by no means so specialized. This early Miocene Ape has been called *Proconsul*,

[1] Pilbeam and Simons (41).
 Simons, E. L. (48) and an important article by Pilbeam (40).

because he was thought to be the forerunner of the chimpanzee—and a very famous chimpanzee in the London Zoo at that time was known as *Consul*. Some authorities regard *Proconsul* as ancestral both to man and the anthropoid apes.

Proconsul was indeed very probably ancestor to the chimpanzee and the gorilla, and reveals a great many unique features in the few skeletal remains that have been discovered. These consist of the almost complete skull and jaw of an ape slightly smaller than the chimpanzee.

Proconsul is an undoubted ape, but an ape different from those now living in several respects. Many of the specializations of present-day chimpanzees have not yet appeared. For instance, their limb structure suggests that the brachiating habit had not been completely adopted. Proconsul seems to have retained rather more of the terrestrial quadrupedal habits of the ordinary monkey. Even the largest forms of this species were lightly built, active creatures compared with modern apes.[1]

Proconsul is a representative of a large group of Miocene Apes (Dryopithecus) found in Asia, Africa and elsewhere, whose fossil forms range from 14,000,000 to 17,000,000 years ago. Most came to a dead end, but one branch gave rise to chimpanzees and gorillas, and quite another, the Far Eastern form, probably evolved into the Orangutan.

By this time, the diverging line of *Hominidae* had reached the level of a type found in Tanzania by Leakey, and called *Kenyapithecus* (also represented by *Ramapithecus* in India and Africa). It is to be noted that among other characteristics, and certainly the most important diagnostically, the dental arcade in *Propliopithecus*, *Kenyapithecus*, and many millions of years later in *Australopithecus* and man, is *rounded* like a horseshoe and the canines much reduced, whereas in the *Pongidae* the shape of the jaw is an elongated rectangle and the canines, even in the fruit-eating modern apes, are well developed. Moreover the *Hominidae* are always less specialized than the *Pongidae*, even less specialized than *Proconsul*, who has not yet reached the brachiated[2] condition of our modern apes.

The point which is emerging is that the *Hominidae* and their ancestors were as unspecialized as every other evolutionary line was

---

[1] Le Gros Clark, W. E. and Leakey, L. S. B. (30).
[2] *Brachiated*—The arms, chest and musculature highly specialized for progress through the branches of trees.

specialized, *including the apes*. Now once the line leading to specialization has been taken no further progress is possible beyond the successful achievement of that highly modified type. As Huxley says "One of the concomitants of organic progress has been the progressive cutting down of the possible modes of further progress, until now all future progress depends on man alone."[1] It was precisely because man's ancestors did *not* specialize that they could go on. Their development did *not* end, as all specializations do, in a dead end. The great majority of biological stock shows no progress, and sometimes even regresses like the parasites. What usually happens is either a dead stop such as the arrest of further development away back in the age of molluscs or arthropods (lobsters, crabs), or, avoiding that fate, a successful development towards the vertebrates. Here again all the *specialized* lines but one can get no farther—the fish, the reptile, the bird are perfect of their kind and finished. Progress continues through an unspecialized line of reptiles to the mammal, a most successful kind of animal: warm blooded, an excellent circulation, the young developing safe inside the mother, and not lying about in succulent eggs. This group becomes dominant and fans out into a great variety of highly specialized orders from kangaroos and elephants to whales and tigers, all adapted to their different environment.

> "Let us take a closer look at the great horde of Pliocene animals—those limbs developed to the last degree of simplicity and perfection, those forests of antlers on the heads of stags . . . those heavy tusks on the snouts of the proboscidians, those canines and incisors of the great carnivores . . . Surely such luxuriance, such achievement, must precisely serve to condemn the future of these magnificent creatures . . . writing them off . . . as forms that have got into a morphological dead end."[2]

The trouble with specialization is that it is irreversible. There is no going back. You can only get better and better at what your whole anatomical set-up is built to do—fly if you are a bird or a bat, burrow if you are a mole, crop herbage if you are a cow. Specialization

> "imprisons the animal that undergoes it in a restricted path at the end of which . . . it runs the risk of ending up either in monstrosity or in fragility. Specialization paralyses,

[1] Huxley, Julian (24), p. 572.
[2] Teilhard de Chardin, P. (52), pp. 155-157.

ultra-specialization kills. Palaeontology is littered with such catastrophes."[1]

Specialization begins a long way back. The ants reached their evolutionary limit 30,000,000 years ago and have hardly changed since.

"When along any line the biochemical limits have been reached, the trend ceases, and the stock, if not extinguished is merely held by selection to the point it has reached . . . A specialized line thus finds itself at the bottom of a groove cut for it by selection—the farther specialization has proceeded, the deeper will be the groove in which it has entrenched itself."[2]

No new *genera* have been formed for millions of years. It is only new *species* that have recently evolved—(e.g. we have different *species* of ducks, but they are all ducks). This process has also slowed down, until today we get different *varieties* of butterflies or birds, either owing to a group being isolated and producing new forms, the difference often being nonadaptive (that is not indicating improvement), or due to some minor adjustment to the environment as when moths on trees in the Midlands become black for protective colouration. "This minor systematic diversity," says Huxley, "has little to do with the major process of evolutionary change" that produced the marvellous adaptations to totally different environments which has virtually come to an end.

The layman may not realize how slowly biological evolution works. In the evolution of the horse, which included a remarkable lengthening of the teeth to crop the coarse prairie grasses, this increase in length was only 1% in a million years. To produce a new genus of the horse family took $7\frac{1}{2}$ million years. In 80 million years the line leading to the opossum changed less than did the horse in 60 million years. The King Crab has not changed for 200 million years. In the last million years no new genus of mammals has appeared and many have disappeared entirely. They would disappear even faster if they were not artificially preserved. Man is the only really successful type, and has remained as a single inter-breeding species and has not radiated out as all other mammals have into a number of biologically separated groups.

[1] *Op. cit.*, p. 159.
[2] Huxley, Julian (24), p. 500.

Only man continues his evolutionary trend, but this is not to any significant extent a matter of further *bodily* change. It is on the contrary a new kind of evolutionary change, the development of technology and civilization, and of the successively different types of *culture*, each giving rise to man of a different character with his own type of habits, ideas, moral rules and so on. These things are not built-in like the modifications of animals, but *learned*, in the mind, passed on by tradition, while the body and brain remain the same.

Man's evolution, says Huxley,

"is not biological but sociological. It operates by the mechanism of cultural tradition which involves the cumulative
self-reproduction and self-variation of mental activities and
their products."[1]

The same position is taken by Professor Waddington who declares that

"evolution has in mankind been reduced to relative un-
importance by the development of a new and characteristically human method of advance—a new capacity for dealing
with environment, achieved not by genetical changes—
for instance, the ability to fly—which man has achieved
not by means of the same biological processes as were
involved when the ancestors of birds developed that
capacity, but by technological invention."[2]

Man has produced a new mechanism which brings about alteration in his relations with the rest of the world; this is of course the development of technology and improved forms of social and economic organization; a method which operates quite differently from and enormously quicker than that on which biological evolution depends.

But this is only possible on the basis of the long process of evolutionary development of the physical organism leading up to man, keeping away from specialized organs, and gradually setting free the hands and enlarging the brain, while developing the possibility not given to any ape of standing, balanced, on the feet with the hands quite free to manipulate.[3] No ape can do this. Every living ape is a quad-

---

[1] Huxley, J. S. (26), p. 16.
[2] Waddington, C. H. (61), p. 101.
[3] We do not call hands specialized, because they can function in an infinitely variable way. In the mole the hands *are* specialized; they have become *spades* and nothing else; and in the bird parts of the wings, nothing else—*that* is specialization.

ruped and goes on all fours on the ground; and every ape has hands on the ends of his legs, not feet!

It is therefore precisely because man did not either descend from a specialized ape or become one that he became a man. Let us see exactly how this happened.

MAN STANDS ALONE

Man's ancestors were tree dwellers who learned to use their hands and eyes to an unusual degree. Then they descended to the ground and learned to run. Another group also descended, but before the arms and hands were well developed, and they remained quadrupeds—the baboons. Man's ancestors, descending later however, perfected the foot and the ability to run and stand. The different and divergent line of the apes remained in the trees, developed enormous arms, tiny legs, huge chests, and thus reached the specialized condition known as *brachiation*. In man the long arms of the ape, and the short legs equipped with hands rather than feet, give way to short arms and long straight legs with flat soled feet and a great toe which cannot, like a thumb, be separated from the rest (as it can be in the apes). The face is small and short and, while prognathous, is not a snout. There is an enormous brain case twice the size of a gorilla's. The teeth plan forms a horseshoe, with the canines no higher than the rest. There is a very definite chin.

Man is not a tree-dweller, the apes are. Man stands easily on flat-soled feet, leaving the hands free to grasp and manipulate: the apes stand best when they pull themselves up by holding on to an overhead bough. They are really still quadrupeds.

The hand shows a great improvement on that found in the ape, the thumb having a much wider range of movements and being nearer the fingers—the ape's thumb appears to be half way down its wrist. The foot is totally different, the first digit (or big toe) being bound across to the metatarsals by a ligament (whereas in the ape it is quite free like a thumb). The legs, of course, are now longer than the arms, whereas in the Orangutan the arms almost reach the ground. The vertebral column, which has the typical human curve, is so placed that standing upright the spinal cord enters the skull from *underneath*, so that man looks forward. In a dog it enters from *behind* so that, if the head is not bent down, an upright position (i.e. if the dog is walking on his hind legs) points the head straight up.

Teeth and jaws have given way to hands for holding things and for fighting and hunting, thus making possible increase of flexibility of the mouth to allow for speech.

Vision, of course, is stereoscopic, and the visual centres in the brain are far larger than those areas connected with the olfactory organs.

Brain size now increases enormously to keep pace with the capacity to manipulate and to make and use tools. This is crucial; a large ape without weapons and tools is biologically speaking an impossibility. The necessary minimum brain capacity of a primitive man would be about 800 c.c. The gorilla reaches 650 c.c. and *Australopithecus* about the same. *Pithecanthropus* reaches 914 c.c., well below the average of any modern human type, which varies between 1,200 and 1,500 c.c.

How shall we describe the first man? He stands on his feet and his hands are quite free. His fingers and thumbs are capable of a kind of manipulation impossible to the ape. He has the stereoscopic vision that enables him to judge near distances, from a foot upwards. And with all this he has a brain not merely larger but capable of mental operations quite impossible to the ape, above all capable of learning to speak. Man alone can keep his eyes fixed on what his hands are doing and so can concentrate. Unlike the ape he can keep seeing things within the range of his moving hands whatever his posture may be. Apes can manipulate to a certain extent when seated but only man can do so freely while standing on his feet. Manual precision involves keeping one's eye on the ball and not having to think about balancing precariously on one's feet like a dog on his hind legs.

The possibility of the manufacture and use of tools depends on the binocular vision developed by the tree-climbing monkeys and lemurs, without which they could not possibly leap so accurately from bough to bough, and later on the upright posture setting the arms completely free. To this must be added the delicate sense of touch for which the fingers and even more the finger tips have been especially built. In this sense of touch man far exceeds the sensitiveness of any animal.

The brain has enlarged in front of the central groove and

the broad belt of cortex associated with muscular action. This appears to be associated with anticipation, planning, and the centres concerned with the co-ordination of the eyes and the articulation of words. The jaws are no longer used to hold things with or to fight with. The huge, long protuberances on the skull for the once powerful muscles disappear and the mouth becomes flexible enough to speak with.

Associated with this is an important and necessary drop in position of the larynx during human evolution. In all mammals prior to man the opening of the larynx normally lies (in the position of rest) above the soft palate and therefore in the cavity of the nose. This allows the animal to breathe while swallowing, but it effectively prevents any elaborate vocalization. The same anatomical situation is present in a newborn baby[1] where it is of obvious advantage. Speech, however, becomes possible in the child only when the larynx drops to below the level of the cavity of the mouth: sound-waves set in motion by the vocal cords can then be manipulated within the mouth-cavity to produce the great variety of sounds associated with speech.

It is interesting to see how the hand preceded the brain in this development. *Australopithecus*, the earliest known precursor of man, whose fossil remains were found in South East Africa, has excellent feet, an upright position, well developed hands, *but a small brain* of 500 c.c. capacity. The hand of the lowest savage can perform hundreds of operations that no monkey's hand can imitate. The opposable thumb, capable of precision grip, is a hominid not a pongid characteristic. After its appearance in *Australopithecus* it improved rapidly by biological mutations which were of considerable survival value, but *only because they were taken advantage of* and used. They were used because the brain was capable of a considerable range of manipulation given a suitable prehensile organ—a hand. This development now alters everything the animal does and its new mode of life requires and selects still further bodily modifications. It is only then, under the pressure of the new demands of a new mode of life and new activities, that brain modifications are of enormous value in enabling the *new* manipulations to be developed and improved. Hence the slightest chance variation in brain size and efficiency is selected and inherited. The effective agencies were thus the brain *and* the hand, itself dependent upon the developed foot, making a firm standing position possible, and thus setting the hands free.

[1] Towers, Bernard (59)

By 500,000 years ago the brain had doubled its size and the first true man *Homo erectus* was lighting fires, making flint implements and living in caves in the vicinity of Pekin (and also in Java and possibly elsewhere).

The brain had still a good way to go, from 1,100 c.c. in *Homo erectus* to 1,500 c.c. in modern man, *Homo sapiens*, but the important leap was from the 500 c.c. of *Australopithecus* (and the Gorilla) to the 1,100 c.c. of *Homo erectus*. This marks the crossing of the line between animal and man.

We must distinguish between the succession of stages in the evolution of the brain and its functions. There are first of all a series of steps forming the basis of simple built-in reactions, and later of a considerable capacity for modification with experience. All these are genetically determined, and the mechanism for response—the 'instructions'—are transmitted by heredity.

But in man we reach a new stage, that of non-genetical transmission by brains that allow us to *teach* and to *learn*. This is a new form of heredity not based on chromosomes but on *learned information*, passed on by tradition. It is the defining characteristic of human beings and has been operating for about 300,000 years. Alfred Lotka distinguishes between what he calls *endosomatic* or internal heredity, transmission by the genetical constitution as with other animals; and *exosomatic* or external heredity that is mediated through tradition. This social, cultural and technological evolution must be sharply distinguished from the genetical form, which for Morris and his associates is the only form taken into account. As Medawar says, nothing could be more foolish or dangerous than to attempt to transfer a purely genetical interpretation of behaviour upon the newer, nongenetical evolution of mankind, which is exactly what they are doing.

"We can jettison all reasoning based upon the idea that changes in society happen in the style and under the pressures of ordinary genetic evolution; abandon any idea that the direction of social change is governed by laws other than laws which have at some time been the subject of human decisions or acts of mind."[1]

It therefore misses the point entirely to say, as Morris does, that the period of civilization has not been long enough "to make any substantial difference to man's genetical make-up". The changes in

[1] Medawar, P. B. (34), p. 99.

human behaviour are not genetical but social, not *endosomatic* but *exosomatic*.

The appearance of true Man thus alters the direction of evolution. It lifts progress onto a new level. Huxley points out that the cerebral hemispheres in vertebrate evolution have increased from zero in the fish to a mass which exceeds all the rest of the nervous system together.

> "The result has been almost as abrupt as the change from solid ice to liquid water . . . This organ of ultimate adjustment and control can rearrange the patterns of experience and action in a far greater variety, and can escape from the particular to the general. By the provision of association mechanisms any activity of the mind can be brought into relation with any other."[1]

It is the mechanism for confronting, weighing and choosing between alternatives in the light of reason and past experience. It is evolution's subjective component. Progress from now on will not come about without human choice, human effort and human purpose.

Only man has crossed the barrier to the higher level and is now not acted upon by biological pressure to move ahead physically or in any other way, but is himself the agent of evolution.

"Within the period of recorded history we can detect only slight indications of biological evolution in human potentialities," but we are confronted with overwhelming evidence of most striking changes in human culture and this in man himself.[2]

Social evolution is proceeding in every decade at a faster and faster rate; and while this is not in any way dependent upon physiological or anatomical changes, which establish themselves exceedingly slowly and do not affect social evolution to any significant step, it has simultaneously changed the character of man to an enormous degree.

What distinguishes man, then, from the animals is this form of development which transcends all genetically inherited animal characteristics and takes charge of these, utilizing them, modifying them and dominating them, until they can be virtually disregarded as having any *independent* influence upon behaviour.

> "Man is the only animal species that, from the very moment he came into existence, has been continuously changing,

[1] Huxley, J. S. (25), pp. 21 and 249.
[2] Waddington, C. H. (61).

and during this process has become a different being."[1]

We make a fundamental mistake if we imagine a native of Tiero del Fuego or Central Africa before the impact of the West as really the same as ourselves. He is not, he is a different man, not physically but mentally, socially, as far as his values and morals and character are concerned. In the animal world a new species remains unchanged except for the varieties which may supervene. We may still find species which are identical with their fossil remains of hundreds of thousands or even millions of years ago. Only man has a continuous *history*, goes through the transformation of historical, social and personal change.

Man from the geological point of view began his effective life and culture not more than 50,000 years ago. "A new thing, a tool . . . a stone shaped by and for the human hand, and a new animal sound, voices, talking."[2] Expressed in a reduced time scale of a few decades for the evolution of the animal world and a few weeks for the bodily origin of man, civilization would have originated little more than an hour ago and the industrial transformation of man and earth would have taken a couple of minutes.

With the rise of the species *Homo sapiens* a new principle came into the world. It introduced instead of a slow biological development, through inherited genetical changes preserved by natural selection, which is the only kind of change some ethologists can conceive, a fast psychosocial development, of invention and economic and cultural development, increasing in speed within this one persisting species.

[1] Pannekoek, A. (39), p. 88.
[2] Sherrington, C. (47), p. 18.

CHAPTER SIX

The Explosion of Mind

THE MENTAL GAP BETWEEN MAN AND THE ANIMALS

The gap between man and apes is much greater than is usually supposed, because intrigued by aspects of ape behaviour which bear a superficial resemblance to those of man we tend to project familiar human qualities onto these animals. We do the same about animals which quite certainly have no intelligence of the human sort, like wasps. We even project malevolence onto inanimate objects and kick the offending chair we have stumbled over or curse the car that won't start. The gap has been further reduced by minimizing the human qualities of man, that is to say by insisting on thinking of him in terms of animal drives, the libido, the instinct of aggression, 'the ape and tiger within', and so forth (*see Figure 1, page* 93).

The real difference is essentially in the brain, and it is only in the human body, says Huxley, that a brain capable of conceptual thought could have been developed. But the hand, and the whole sequence of parallel anatomical accompaniments, provide the indispensable conditions of this brain development.

What has happened here is that the enlargement of the association areas has led to the appearance of a mechanism by which any activity of the mind can be brought into relation with any other, so that an immense amount of information is *synthesised* and *interiorised* —held in the mind, and consciously associated with past experience and imagined projects, for overcoming the immediate difficulty or deciding on the course to be followed. Always, present and future actions are guided and directed by *ideas* of this sort. It is this complex and integrated mental activity which guides the human species up the paths of progress. We call it the development of conceptual thought, and it is accompanied by the addition of self-consciousness to simple awareness of the environment. Both of these appear in man alone.

Whatever capacity for modifying instinctive behaviour animals have, in man this capacity is raised to a higher power, which is achieved by the appearance of conceptual thought and implies the power of speech.

"Speech makes the leap of symbolic representation whereby it becomes possible, not merely to excite reactions and feelings in others (by animal noises), but to convey ideas . . . From this arises a new layer in evolution."[1]

THE LEVEL OF CONCEPTUAL THOUGHT

Man now abandons the rigidity of instinct for an altogether new plasticity, seen in the progressive improvement of tools; and, accompanying this, another method of coping with problems, and using the tools, i.e. planned co-operative ventures of a kind utterly unknown to the animal. Two things accompany this: (a) speech, which is inseparable from conceptual thought; and (b) the cumulative transmission of knowledge. *Speech* involves symbols for classes of objects and classes of actions, not merely expressions of emotion as in animals. To have words for objects as members of a class provides the potential basis for the concept. *Knowledge* follows as the development of a cumulative tradition. Animals learn, but there is no cumulative knowledge. Each animal starts afresh; and we never get beyond the gap of one generation. Man proceeds along the path of indefinite improvement. Lord Brain calls this "transcendence by mind of the life of individual man". It is followed by writing and then by printing; it leads to the establishment of social cultures, moulding the lives of their members and exhibiting their own phases of growth and change.

It is generally agreed that once this leap to the potentialities of modern man was effected, as seen first in Cromagnon man in Late Palaeolithic times (about 40,000 years ago), a level was reached which

---

[1] Brain, Russell (10), p. 60.

offers possibilities by no means realized even yet.

Man's mental powers have not changed since then by reason of any further development of the brain, though he has changed himself immensely by successive advances in technology, social organization and political structure.

> "Evolution has since that date overtly overflowed its anatomical modalities to spread, or perhaps even . . . to transplant itself, into the zones of psychic spontaneity both individual and collective."[1]

From now on the influence of mental factors outweighs by far the variations of ever-dwindling bodily changes. As Cassirer says,

> "The new acquisition transforms the whole of human life. As compared with the other animals man lives not merely in a broader reality; he lives, so to speak, in a new dimension of reality."[2]

For this reason, educability is a species character of man,

> "which confers upon him the unique position which he holds in the animal kingdom. Its acquisition freed him from the constraint of a limited range of biologically predetermined responses. He became capable of acting in a more or less regulative manner upon his physical environment instead of being largely regulated by it. Man's suppleness, plasticity, and most important of all, ability to profit by experience and education are unique. No other species is comparable in its capacity to acquire new behaviour patterns and discard old ones in consequence of training."[3]

Instead of having his responses fixed as in other animal species, man is a species that invents its own responses, and it is out of this unique ability to invent and improvise his response that his cultures are born.

INTELLIGENCE

Animals have a limited kind of intelligence which is completely

---

[1] Teilhard de Chardin, P. (52), p. 202.
[2] Cassirer, E. (12).
[3] Montagu, Ashley (35), p. 48.

separate from that found in man. Whatever their capacity to extend
and modify instinctual behaviour, it never reaches the level of free
ideas. It remains at what animal psychologists call the *perceptual* and
not the rational level.

The *extension* and improvement of instinctual behaviour may
be (a) by conditioning (b) by acquirements of skill by practice (c) by
habits, and (d) by learning through success and failure. Beyond this
some animals can solve very simple problems like pulling up a worm
that has been attached to a string (birds), fitting sticks together, or
climbing on boxes to reach food (apes). But psychologists do not
regard this as an explicit understanding of causal relations.[1] It remains
on the level of instinctive activity; as does the simple use of thorns,
sticks, small stones and so forth by ants, wasps and birds for whom
these articles appear to be no more than an extension of limb, jaws
or beak.

The psychologists hold that the animal sees only the total
perceptual setup including the 'tool', and jumps to the possibility. It
takes place on the level of *concrete* understanding. It is not using concepts, recalling the past or anticipating the future. It does not pass
beyond the level of perception, or direct sensorial insight. It is more a
'seeing' than a 'thinking'. Bierens de Haan concludes,

"There is a broad rift between animals and man. On one
side stands the animal, a creature living in the world of
the perceptual, the concrete, on the other side stands man,
living in both that world and the world of the conceptual,
of general ideas."[2]

A distinction is therefore drawn between the kind of learning
that is definitely a stage higher than simple trial and error learning
and marks a new level in intelligence, and the still higher level,
only found in man, concerned with the apprehension of relations.[3] At
the level of perceptual learning not all the possible solutions are attempted because the animal now has what are called 'learning sets',
or patterns of solutions each of which can be applied to a number of
similar problems.[4] But at this level, we still have only a behavioural
solution of the problem.

With the development of the cerebral cortex which takes

[1] Bierens de Haan (8) and Thorpe, W. H. (55), Chapter V.
[2] *Op. cit.*, p. 146.
[3] Klopfer & Hailman (28).
    Blough, D. S. and P. M. (9) and Barnett, S. A. (4).

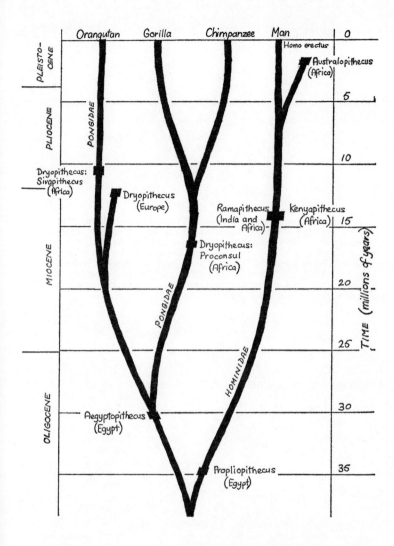

Figure I

Genealogical tree of Man, Australopithecus and the anthropoid apes, as far as can be inferred from the fossil evidence at present available. The scheme follows Le Gros Clark (*The Antecedents of Man*), incorporating the recent researches of Pilbeam (*Science Journal* Feb. 1967). The link between Propliopithecus and Kenyapithecus is problematical. Earlier authorities put the divergence of Hominidae and Pongidae at 16,000,000 years ago. Pilbeam is inclined to put it much earlier.

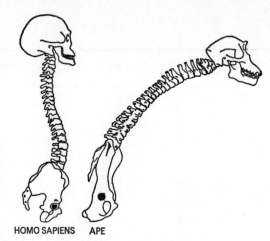

HOMO SAPIENS   APE

Figure 2

Comparison of skull, spinal column and pelvis of ape and man, which shows the entry of the spinal cord far back in the ape, and well forward in man. Similarly in man the spinal column balances the skull, supporting it centrally, while the column is well behind in the ape, requiring powerful neck muscles to hold the head up. Note the great difference in the pelvic girdle, which serves quadrupedal gait in the ape, but the erect posture, upright walking, and running in man. After Boule and Vallois (1957), and Clark (1967).

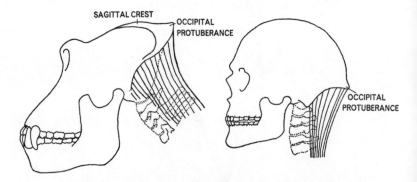

Figure 3

Contrast between pongid and hominid skulls. Note the massive neck muscles in the gorilla, attached right up to the occipital protuberance. This is necessary to hold the head up because the spinal column articulates with the back of the skull. In man the occipital protuberance is very low, since the skull is balanced by the spinal column which articulates centrally. Note also that in man the brain case rises to a considerable height above the orbit, and the skull is rounded back and front. The brain case of the ape is very low and much smaller and flatter. The face in man is *below* the brain case and vertical; in the ape it is not vertical and is almost *in front* of the brain case.

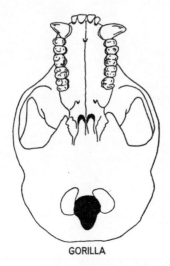

GORILLA

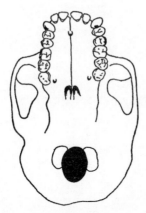

AUSTRALOPITHECUS

Figure 4
Base of skull of gorilla and Australopithecus. Note the rounded arcade of the hominid and the absence of enlarged canines, whereas the pongid palate is rectangular and long, with very powerful canines. The opening for entry of the spinal cord has moved forward. The jaw pattern of the Hominidae can be traced back to Propliopithecus, 35 million years, indicating a possible ancestral type. The characteristic jaw of the Pongidae goes back to Dryopithecus, and in its earliest form is found in Aegyptopithecus, about 30 million years ago.

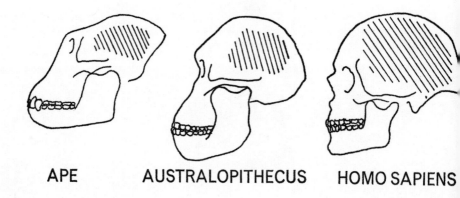

APE   AUSTRALOPITHECUS   HOMO SAPIENS

Figure 5

A comparison of the skulls and brain sizes of ape, Australopithecus and man. The skulls of ape and Australopithecus are already very different (as is the rest of the skeleton), but brain size is about the same in cubic capacity. The human brain is twice this size. (The lateral view, while showing that it is larger, does not indicate the cubic capacity.)

place in the transition to man and reaches in Java Man and Pekin Man the level of human intelligence, we enter an entirely new and qualitatively higher phase.

"New capacities for behaviour emerge in evolution that fall under the general category of reasoning, abstract ability and symbolic process. When these are developed, an organism is freed from slavish dependence on sensory stimulus instinct, or habit, and can make its adaptation to the environment with insight, reasoning, and the use of symbols, and ultimately of language."[1]

The psychologist does not read into the animal's behaviour the experience that he would be having if he (the psychologist) were in the same situation. We must be careful not to project human modes of thought upon typical animal behaviour. The iron law for animal psychologists warns us that "*We must not ascribe an animal's action to some higher psychical process as long as it is possible to describe it as the result of a process which stands lower in the scale of psychical development.*" (Morgan's Principle).

The distinction between the two levels of concrete understanding on the one hand and real intelligence on the other can be accurately determined by means of carefully devised tests. In these tests it is astonishing how completely the most intelligent ape fails to reach the level of a child of two or three in solving test problems.

It becomes clear that what makes the difference is *the general idea*. Children who can talk use the higher form of problem solving and use words. Children who can't, behave like apes. Apes behave very like mentally defective children. A normal child of three can grasp situations that are far too complex for a chimpanzee's mind, and can invent solutions that involve elaborate rearrangements. The real dividing line is clearly the possession of conceptual thought and speech.[2]

Osman Hill draws the same conclusion and points out that no ape has ever developed a culture. Not even the most elementary culture exhibited by surviving savages serves to bridge the gap separating anthropoid psychology from that which is undeniably human.[3]

Huxley adds the important idea that man alone has also

---

[1] Dethier and Stellar (14), p. 72.
[2] Viaud, Gaston (60), p. 53.
[3] Osman Hill, W. C. (38), p. 100.

G

entered the realm where things and experiences can have a value in themselves. Such standards of value applied to forms of conduct, and covering all the different kinds of conduct belonging to that form, demand conceptual thought. Nothing approaching this is found in any ape or dog or horse. This is not to say that animals cannot be taught by conditioning to refrain from doing things that we dislike, by associating the behaviour we wish to eliminate with some kind of pain or deprivation. By similar means we can teach them to do as we desire by appropriate rewards. But a conditioned reflex, or a habit, is not a moral choice. The moral concept generates a new framework of universals and ideas; and one of the functions of humanity is its evolutionary experiment in creating such new experiences of value and thus conceiving new goals to pursue.

MAN AND THE INSTINCTUAL LIFE

If man's behaviour has now entered this qualitatively different and higher phase, what has the inherited, instinctual behaviour pattern of apes got to do with it? Nothing at all. These are *alternative* modes of conduct, the one evolving over twenty or thirty million years down one line, and the other down a diverging line of quite different animals, maintaining their unspecialized condition and their own quite different forms of life from that of the tree-living anthropoids. *There is no known pongid (anthropoid ape) bodily form or manner of life in any known ancestor of man.* There is therefore no evidence for there ever having been a similar behaviour pattern,[1] even if such behaviour patterns could be of any significance for their human descendants (*see Figures 2 and 3, page* 94).

Desmond Morris and Ardrey are rather disingenuous on this subject; they repeatedly speak of man's inheritance of such behaviour patterns; and this is the point they wish us to grasp, and which has all too readily been accepted by so many of their readers. But while some very odd sexual habits and some other features of ape behaviour form the most intriguing part of Morris's comparison of men and apes, it is the propensities for aggression which we mainly have in mind, and

---

[1] The genetical inheritance of such complex behaviour patterns as those found in apes has never been demonstrated and would be very difficult to prove. It is an example of a frequently repeated *assumption* of the principle in question.

which tend to persuade people that man has inherited them from his animal ancestors. But Morris and Ardrey know very well that the ape is a vegetarian, not a fighter, not a predator, not a carnivore; not even aggressive or combative if not attacked. But at this point Ardrey (followed here by Morris) changes his argument entirely. Man does not inherit his aggressive instincts from the apes, we are now told, but when descending from the trees, he became a carnivore, a hunter and a killer, "a predator whose natural instinct is to kill with a weapon."[1]

The argument proceeds to claim that this change of bodily form and habit denied the habit of our pacific ape-like ancestors and established genetically this new habit. This is supposed to have happened in the *Australopithecus* period of man's ancestry about a million years ago. Defenders of this position argue that the habit of civilized man, following new methods of social organization and the appearance of human morals, has been established so recently that they have been unable to overcome this inherited propensity to kill, because there has not been time "to make any substantial difference to man's genetical make-up".

This argument first of all assumes that hunting carries with it a genetically established propensity to aggression against one's fellows. There is not the slightest evidence that this is so. Secondly, that civilized man can only overcome any such propensity by wiping out the old heredity and establishing an hereditary pattern of good behaviour. Now we know no geneticist, no psychologist, and no anthropologist who holds either that the predatory habits of hunters are genetically established or that civilization is attempting to establish new and more acceptable *inherited*, and *genetically based modes of conduct*. The habits of civilized man have developed on the basis of human potentialities, a basic nature, *which is entirely plastic*, so that the new behaviour is not inherited genetically, but established sociologically, culturally, and transmitted by education. The most exhaustive studies that have been made in the habits, morals, values and behaviour of primitive man are all concerned with the sociological and cultural determination of human behaviour.[2] Nothing has been established which would suggest that this is genetically determined, and no one has suggested that it is. In fact the immense diversity of

---

[1] There is not the slightest evidence of man possessing an "instinct to kill with a weapon". No psychologist has ever found such an instinct.
[2] Firth, R. (17), Macbeath, A. (32).

moral behaviour in the world today, from peaceful farmers to head hunters, and amiable fisher folk to the originally surly and quarrelsome Manus, rules out the genetical determination of human behaviour.

This has been strongly supported by the *Statement on the Nature of Race and Race Differences* issued by the Conference of Physical Anthropologists and Geneticists called by UNESCO (September 1952). After declaring that:

> Available scientific knowledge provides no basis for believing that the groups of mankind differ in their innate capacity for intellectual and emotional development,

and further elaborating the case against claiming superiority for any race, they went on to say that there was no scientific evidence to

> justify the conclusion that inherited genetic differences are a major factor in producing the differences between the cultures and cultural achievements of different peoples.

What does determine such diversities of behaviour patterns is not the genetical factor but "the cultural experience which each group has undergone." The intellectual and moral life being conditioned by training and by the particular social environment.

They further pointed out that the vast social changes in such nations or groups as the Greeks, the Arabs, the Scandinavians, in historic times

> "have not been connected in any way with changes in racial type. Historical and sociological studies thus support the view that genetic differences are of little significance in determining the social and cultural differences between different groups of men."

What is equally important is the rapidity of change in fundamental behaviour. It is sometimes suggested that 10,000 years is all too short a time to establish a genetically different kind of character. If character were so determined this would be so; for, as we saw, to secure an increase of 1% in the length of a horse's tooth took a million years. But in fact only a thousand years ago the peaceful Danish farmers were blood-thirsty pirates. We know that the great Islamic culture of the years 700 to 1,200 A.D. declined into the backward Turkish Empire of the 19th century. We remember the decadence of Greece, of Egypt, of Italy following the Renaissance. Margaret Mead describes the complete reversal of character in the Manus of

New Guinea within 25 years, originally a quarrelsome and ill-disposed tribe; many observers of these people came to regard them as permanently cast into this mould, and deeply inbred with a rather unpleasant kind of 'original sin'. But changes in social and political organization, in religion and moral beliefs, resulted in a striking change, from the appearance of the villages, to changes of customs, ceremonial, marriage relationships and personality. They became friendly instead of harshly competitive, relaxed and unworried instead of anxious, irascible, bad-tempered and aggressive.[1]

We conclude from this comparison of the evolutionary process in animals and man, that beyond the period of man's emergence human evolution has proceeded on entirely different lines from the genetical processes which produced him. The theories advanced by Morris and Ardrey appear to be without scientific foundation:

1 There is no evidence of a neurological or psychological nature to warrant the transmission of the behaviour patterns of apes to man, with his enormous brain with its 10,000 million neurones and totally new structures and capacities, compared with the brain of contemporary apes and indeed the whole *Pongidae* family going back for more than 20 million years (*see Figure 5, page* 96).

2 On the contrary, while most animal behaviour patterns are inherited and instinctual and are virtually complete at birth, and are only slightly modified by conditioning and perceptual learning, most human behaviour is based on simple, non-specific needs and propensities, which develop as learned behaviour based on conceptual thinking, and, far from reaching the limits of modification found in animals (based on conditioning, etc.), is without limits in its possibility of change, developments and radical transformation.

3 There is not the slightest evidence for primitive man, either *Homo sapiens*, or his immediate progenitor *Homo erectus*, or his earlier ancestors the Australopithecenes, being instinctive killers, driven by the congenital urge to destroy or dominate his fellows.

4 There is no evidence at all about the habits of fossil man to

[1] Mead, Margaret (33).

support Ardrey's theory. Modern man is known to behave in an immense variety of ways, but the more primitive he is the more co-operative and less aggressive he appears to be. There is no evidence for warlike behaviour before 40,000 years ago; war reaches the level of mass slaughter or enslavements not before the Bronze Age.

CHAPTER SEVEN

The Path of Progress

There is, we see, not one evolutionary road, but two: the biological road of genetical variation and slow adaptation to the environment—an immensely slow process, which in every direction but one leads to close adaptation to environmental pressure, and stability when that kind of success is won. The other—when evolution has produced in man a capacity for *dealing with the environment* rather than adapting the organism to it, which, compared with genetic change, is both extremely rapid and far reaching. This liberates him from the method of chance variation and the slow modification of the bodily mechanism. Now he begins to control the physical world and build successive cultural systems based on a developing technology. As he does so he reorganizes his social life to make it as effective as possible in getting human betterment from the new methods of production. By remaking society in these ways he, of course, remakes himself, as Professor Gordon Childe shows in his vivid sketch of the formation of human society from its earliest beginnings.[1]

Thus "the whole of history", as Marx once said, "is nothing but the progressive transformation of human nature. By acting on the world and changing it, man changes his own nature."

If we turn to Dobzhansky, the leading geneticist of human evolution,[2] we shall find a complete endorsement of the views of Huxley and Waddington which we have been discussing; "we are

[1] Childe, V. Gordon (13).
[2] Dobzhansky, T. (15) and (16).

dealing", he says,

"with the emergence of a whole new evolutionary pattern,
a transition to a novel way of life which is human rather
than animal . . . Man is not simply a very clever ape."[1]

Thus man cannot be seen as reflecting in his behaviour a fixed set of
human drives; all his instinctual behaviour, which in any case consists
of only a very few fundamental impulses like sex and feeding and
gregariousness, are intertwined with and absorbed into learned reactions; so that while in animals behaviour is predominantly instinctual, in man it is almost entirely a product of culture, imparted by
teaching and learning. Comparing the character of men living in ancient
Egypt or under the medieval European monarchies with the same races
today, Dobzhansky sees a total transformation, and declares that most of

"these changes evidently occurred not because human populations were altered genetically, but because they were
altered culturally. The human species is biologically an
extraordinary success, precisely because its culture can
change ever so much faster than its gene pool. This is the
reason cultural evolution has become adaptively the most
potent extension of biological evolution. For at least 10,000
or perhaps for 1,000,000 years man has been adapting his
environments to his genes more often than his genes to his
environments. And the supremacy of culture in adaptation
doubtless will continue in the foreseeable future. In this
sense, but in this sense only, it may be said that man has
escaped from the clutches of his biological past and has
become to some extent the master, rather than the slave,
of his genes."[2]

Far-reaching cultural transformations have manifestly taken
and are taking place. Do genetic changes accompany the cultural
ones? White believes that

"in the man-culture equation over a period of a million
years, we may assume some absolute increase in the magnitude of the biological factor. But during the last hundred or
even the last fifty thousand years we have no evidence of
an appreciable increase in mental ability."[3]

[1] Dobzhansky, T. (15), p. 199.
[2] *Op. cit.*, p. 319.
[3] White, L. A. (62).

"The assumption of the psychic unity, or uniformity, of mankind is probably pivotal in the working philosophy of a majority of anthropologists, psychologists, sociologists, and of not a few biologists. They maintain that biological evolution has achieved the genetic basis of culture and run its course; it is now a matter of the past. The genetic basis of culture is uniform everywhere; cultural evolution has long since taken over."[1]

INNATE CHARACTER AND RACISM

The belief that racial differences indicating both superiority and inferiority, and also natural differences, which may indicate aggressiveness, a militaristic nature, laziness, energy, lethargy, or initiative, are innate in various nations, tribes and races, is now entirely obsolete among geneticists and anthropologists. These characteristics are now regarded, as we have seen, as basically cultural.[2]

AGGRESSION IN HUMAN CHARACTER

Our inheritance from hypothetical aggressive animal ancestors is frequently supposed to constitute in man a heritage of evil, described by Tennyson as 'the Ape and Tiger' within us, 'the yelp of the beast'. As one broadcaster put it, "evil wells up from the abysmal depth of the corrupt heart of man", a view which echoes old ideas of man's original sin. Anthony Storr, whom we may quote again, concludes a depressing paragraph on man's innate wickedness by declaring that "we know in our hearts that each one of us harbours within himself the same savage impulses which lead to murder, to torture and to war."[3]

Defenders of the views we are criticizing will declare, of course, that although human behaviour is not unalterable, "man's self-control of it is likely to be more effective the more he can understand the nature of its inherited base." But in what way could we

---

[1] Dobzhansky, T. (15), p. 320.
[2] Ruth Benedict has applied these principles to the contrasting natural characteristics, particularly as concerning claims to racial superiority appearing in history, in her book, RACE AND RACISM. (5).
[3] Storr, Anthony (51), Introduction, p. ix.

control it better for this knowledge? Men have for centuries believed this sort of thing; it is for all practical purposes the same as the doctrine of original sin, but the repressive steps taken to quell 'the beast within', the resort to moral exhortation or divine grace, has not proved effective. And for a very good reason—there is no evidence of any such *biological* origin for man's iniquity. Even animal aggression (a relatively rare occurrence in nature, for even Lorenz declares that predatory animals hunting their prey show no signs of anger), may be better accounted for by frustration, by such abnormal circumstances as overcrowding, or other environmental and psychological causes. Biologists are themselves ruling out the idea of a self-stimulating aggressive system in animals, and placing the emphasis on environmental abnormalities. If not in animals, why in man? If we take this conclusion along with the well established fact of man's behaviour being essentially cultural and not genetically determined, the lesson to be derived would seem to be that there is no instinctive aggressive drive in man; in which case it is far more likely to have an environmental and social origin. In that case it would certainly be possible to lessen the likelihood of interpersonal conflict by decreasing the occurrence of frustrations and providing more opportunities for satisfying basic needs through co-operation.

This is the view of many psychologists. Professor Flugel in his MAN, MORALS AND SOCIETY, shows the many ways in which faults in education and parental upbringing are responsible for character faults. Karen Horney, the American psychoanalyst, says that among business men neurosis arises out of the anxieties which beset them in a competitive society. This can produce neurotic trends such as aggression on the one hand or extreme timidity on the other. From this trend is derived the tough type, the rugged individualist, who though he regards himself (and is regarded by others) as being typical of human nature, is actually inhibiting his capacity for friendship, love, sympathetic understanding and co-operation. Moreover, beneath this aggressive front is invariably the component of fear, never admitted or displayed.[1]

According to Fromm, it is not the neurotic condition which is responsible for the sickness of our acquisitive society; on the contrary, it is the social situation which gives rise to the neurosis.[2]

[1] Horney, Karen (22), p. 64.
[2] Fromm, Erich (19).

Ian Suttie, in his ORIGINS OF LOVE AND HATE (London 1935), denies the existence of a basic aggressive characteristic of natural man, antecedent to the formation of society and responsible for society being little more than police-regulated, possessive individualism, as though what moral qualities we achieve are won *against* the state of nature. Suttie finds on the contrary an inherent sociality without which individuals would not survive. This is a primary relationship of recognized mutual independence which arises on the basis of work—work implying, necessarily, such co-operation. Aggression he sees as a secondary reaction, resulting from the thwarting of human needs.

The Russells have also come to the conclusion that aggression is a response to social stress and is not innate. Their recent study of violence in monkeys and man indicates that primates are under natural conditions peaceable. It is only in abnormal circumstances such as shortage of food or overcrowding that struggle breaks out. They conclude that since it appears to be the case among animals that when all needs are satisfied we get peaceful societies, then similar conditions should produce peaceful societies among men.[1]

It is unnecessary to create an entity such as 'aggression', conceived as some ineradicable biological urge, if the phenomena concerned can quite simply be explained without it.

Berkowitz takes a very similar position:

"Since 'spontaneous' animal aggression is a relatively rare occurrence in nature (and there is the possibility that even these infrequent cases may be accounted for by frustration), many ethologists and experimental biologists rule out the possibility of a self-stimulating aggressive system in animals. One important lesson to be derived from these studies is that there is no instinctive drive towards war in man."[2]

If this view of man's nature is correct it should certainly be possible to lessen the likelihood of interpersonal conflict by decreasing the occurrence of frustrations.

This has been convincingly demonstrated in a study of the causes of conflict on the North West Frontier of India. On the barren hills of this region, on which nothing will grow, live the Pathan tribes. For a century and a half the British Army endeavoured, fruitlessly, to restrain the 'aggression' of these tribesmen. Below were the fruitful

[1] Russell, C. & W. M. S., VIOLENCE, MONKEYS AND MAN (1968). Not in *Bibliography*.
[2] Berkowitz, L. (6), pp. 24 and 25.

plains; what could be expected but that the mountain tribesmen would resort to plundering incursions in order to obtain the necessities of life? It was environment that shaped the character of the Pathans, not inherited instinct. Why could we not have attempted something like the vast irrigation projects carried on in the adjoining Republic of Tadjikistan, just over the mountains, where in exactly similar circumstances racially similar frontier tribes are now living in peace and prosperity?[1]

No one denies that crime, war and aggression are found in human society. The question is whether it is to be attributed to innate hostility, in which case little can be done about it, or to social and psychological causes. The grave fault of all theories of innate wickedness is that they paralyse the mind and will, and reconcile people to a state of affairs which they come to regard as inevitable. The constant attribution of every kind of cruelty and violence, whether within the community, or abroad, or in war and civil war, or revolutionary uprising, whether in social strife or the upsurge of Black Power and its repression, to the ineradicable drive to violence, because man is "only an ape", because he is "a predator and a natural killer", can only have the effect of causing us to regard this as a normal part of human life and of reconciling us to it—even of condoning our own participation.

The theory creates a climate of belief in which violence and cruelty grow, and at the same time prevents our effort to seek for and remove the real causes. If it is all due to inherited instinct, why look any further?

This is one of those questions on which the scientist and the writer who publicise the results of scientific research have a serious responsibility. Literature in every form, and also the theatre and the cinema, cannot but absorb ideas of genetically determined vice, and a heritage of aggression and cruelty derived from our animal ancestors. When this takes the form of widely read novels, and of plays and films seen by thousands, it must have the effect of accustoming people to the idea of man's violence and of leading them to expect nothing better. This can have the effect of actually suggesting to men and women, and to children, that this is what they are like. It can therefore actually encourage behaviour of this kind. A recent review of David Rudkin's play AFORE NIGHT COME, says,

[1] C. Colin Davies, 'The Problem of the North West Frontier', in *The Modern Quarterly*, September, 1949.

"basically the theme is that of LORD OF THE FLIES—the incredible, primitive savagery and blood-lust latent in mankind, so easily brought to the surface, fed by the instinctive fear of what is strange."[1]

Are we really as bad as this? Do the NAKED APE theorists, the dramatists, the novelists and the critics who proclaim these views really feel like this about themselves—or are these evil passions only in the rest of us? One surely finds among children, among ordinary people, among one's friends and neighbours, a vast amount of decency and good feeling. Are our neighbours, the school children we meet, the general run of cheerful young people, as corrupted as we are told? That there is crime, and that there can be violence on a large scale, and cruel wars, is not denied; but specific causes must be sought for this. It does not for a moment appear to be the case that all of us, without exception,

"harbour within ourselves savage impulses which lean to murder, torture and to war",

or that we are all under the sway of "incredible, primitive savagery and blood lust." Did not Shelley more truly speak when he said "There is a spirit within man at enmity with nothingness and desolation". This spirit is not only revealed in the nobler philosophies of our time, but receives the full support of modern science. The real sciences of anthropology, psychology and sociology give us a very different picture from that presented by the disciples of the NAKED APE philosophy.

We may sum up our conclusions thus:

What factors are determinitive of human behaviour if these are not patterns and instincts inherited from our animal ancestors?

(a) The chief determinants of human behaviour are neither anatomical nor genetical. Human habits and customs are not biologically determined and are anything but stereotyped. There is no evidence for unalterable drives for ownership or dominance or to kill.

(b) All that man inherits from his animal ancestors is transformed and penetrated by intelligence and knowledge and does not exist as an instinctive force exerting an irrational compulsion upon his conduct. That is why in man stereotyped behaviour patterns are not inherited.

[1] Review in *Encore* by Tom Milne.

(c) We are thus brought to see the uniqueness of man in spite of his development from the animal level. In nothing is this difference and this uniqueness more clearly manifested than in man's recognition and formulation of principles of value and ethical standards.

This has been very clearly set down by one of our leading ethologists, W. H. Thorpe:

"To assume that studies of animal behaviour imply any decrease in the stature of man would be a view of the utmost naivete . . . Man displays emergent qualities far transcending those of the highest animal. The existence of his high powers of abstract reasoning and his faith, of his religious awareness and spiritual life, his appreciation of moral and aesthetic values, his selfconscious discipline of the will to achieve beauty, goodness and truth; as well as all the other manifestations of his genius that have already emerged, not only confirms this, but suggests that there are also in him vast further potentialities yet to be realised."[1]

THE NEXT DEVELOPMENT IN MAN

One cannot but be convinced by the whole weight of contemporary scientific evidence that man, far from being "A Naked Ape", is a Man, and predestined not to the endless war against his fellows, but to the completion and fulfilment of his nature in human fellowship.

Sir Wilfred Le Gros Clark, in his Presidential Address to the British Association (1961), sees the evolution of man as essentially the achievement and progress of organized social life.

"Consciously directed co-operativeness has been the major factor which has determined the evolutionary origin of *Homo sapiens* as a new emergent species and the gradual development of the peculiarly human form of integrated society. It demanded an accelerated development of those parts of the brain whereby the emotional and instinctual impulses can be more effectively subordinated to the good of the community as a whole. Our task is to give full expression to the deep-rooted altruism which is an essential

[1] Thorpe, W. H. (55), p. 417.

attribute of the humanity of man."

It is this view of man that the world so desperately needs today, not a return to the jungle, and 'the war of all against all'. Yet it is this attitude that has been seized upon by many novelists, feature writers, broadcasters and playwrights, who imagine that they are giving us a scientific picture of man in biological terms, as driven solely by animal instinct. Some of our best modern works of literature have thus been led to depict the dissolution of our world in precisely these terms and they do it with masterly fidelity. They are the eloquent witnesses of a generation whose disillusion has touched bottom. This is an ideology that bears the stamp of that Death Wish which for Freud was only the other side of the coin when we speak of aggression. D. H. Lawrence, when he, in his time, met this kind of thinking, declared: "One must speak for life and growth, amid all this mass of destruction and disintegration." We can surely do so even more effectively when we come to understand that in fact man evolves socially by a very different method than that which the ethologist sees at work, and which obsesses the minds of so many of our modern thinkers and writers. He himself controls the evolution of society by the *choice* of values, by his *preference* for his own forms of social life and cultural good. Not merely survival, but the survival of what is worth having and worth living for becomes his standard; and the kind of stability he seeks is not that of subordination to mere strength or the lowest common denominator of passivity; but a society in which every individual finds the way to the fulfilment of his potentialities in accepting the obligations of fellowship and co-operation. This is a society that continuously lifts itself above the blind competitive struggle in which only the strong survive; a society for which the categorical imperative is "to overthrow all conditions in which man is a humiliated, enslaved, despised and rejected being."

CHAPTER EIGHT

Integration of Past and Future

The popular press seems often to imply that it is only in the present age that man has become sufficiently 'daring' to face the 'stark reality' of his kinship with the rest of nature. The views of those who aim to denigrate and vilify man are being advertised and praised with expressions such as 'takes the lid off our animal nature' or 'allows us to peer through the veil that hides man from the truth about himself'. It is as though no-one in history had ever thought such things before. Of course that is not true. The big difference today, though, is that anyone who can find an outlet in the mass-media—which seem, for the moment, to thrive on scandal and human distress of all kinds—can promulgate his views on a scale never possible in former ages. If the listening-public, reading-public, viewing-public are given no information about the underlying philosophies and prejudices of commentators who purport to speak in the name of science, then they will either accept the views and act on them, or in rejecting them might reject science itself. Both possibilities would be disastrous for civilization. Writers and broadcasters have considerable responsibilities in matters of education and the dissemination of information. Those who promote the 'naked ape' thesis must be held responsible in some measure when their audiences accept and act upon it.

Much of our criticism has been directed, in this book, against some of the professional exponents of the science known as animal ethology. It should be pointed out, in fairness to that scientific discipline, that much the same sort of criticism has been voiced from within its own ranks. The Cambridge Professor of Animal Ethology, Dr. W. H.

Thorpe, F.R.S., recently said:

> "Many scientists and too many philosophers write . . . as if
> they believed that man lacks a 'mind'—a conscious,
> knowing, striving and understanding mind. The absurdity
> of such a view to any person not blinded by too long im-
> mersion in a particular kind of thought-process, is manifest.
> But only too often the experts fail to see how disastrous to
> the ordinary man and perhaps ultimately to civilization itself,
> their views may be if put over in semi-popular language
> incautiously and irresponsibly. Indeed, one feels some-
> times that the clever are simply trying to bamboozle the
> good in order to indulge themselves in the mental titilla-
> tion which results from shocking people."[1]

On the basis of his scientific studies of human and animal behaviour,
Thorpe is convinced[2] of what he calls the uniqueness of man's self-
reflective consciousness, and of his capacity for abstract thought in
anything but the most rudimentary sense. With Teilhard de Chardin,
whose works he often quotes with admiration and approval, he con-
siders that the advent of what Teilhard called the 'noosphere' (the
thinking, or self-reflective 'layer' of life) represents a development in
evolution quite as significant and 'revolutionary' as was the advent of
the 'biosphere' (the 'living layer' of the world) within and from what
was previously inorganic matter.

Thorpe makes many trenchant comments on the shortcom-
ings of reductionist thinking. In protesting about it he is heir to a long
tradition. It is simply not true that the 'naked ape' concept, or the
protests against it, are new phenomena, nor that only modern 'emancipated' man has thought of himself as an ape. At the beginning of the
nineteenth century, some forty years before the publication of Darwin's
ORIGIN OF SPECIES, the implications of Desmond Morris's main thesis
were clearly envisaged by William Lawrence: the famous lectures that
he delivered between 1813-1816 at the Royal College of Surgeons did
much to liberate scientific thinking about man from metaphysical and
theological shackles, and in many ways prepared the ground for
Darwin. Lawrence stood firmly for free and untrammelled enquiry
and for unbiassed objective assessments. Thus he says,

"To discover truth, and to represent it in the clearest and

[1] Thorpe, W. H. (58), p. 48.
[2] See also references 56 and 57.

most intelligible manner, seem to me the only proper objects of physiological, or indeed of any other enquiries. Free discussion is the surest way, not only to disclose and strengthen what is true, but to detect and expose what is fallacious. Let us not then pay so bad a compliment to truth, as to use in its defence foul blows and unlawful weapons."[1]

He was referring here to both the anti-religious prejudices of some authors and the pro-religious prejudices of others. He was equally critical of both.

The interesting thing from our present point of view is that Lawrence was very critical of the ape-man doctrines promulgated by Monboddo and Rousseau. The notion, current for over half a century previously, that men and apes in Africa were really of the same stock, was subjected to scientific scrutiny, and the author concluded:

"I do not hesitate to assert, that the notion of specific identity between the African and orang-outang, is as false, philo-sophically, as the moral and political consequences, to which it would lead, are shocking and detestable."[2]

Today most 'progressives' would join in criticizing the racialist element in the theory, but seem oddly silent when the same idea, extended to include all men, is propounded for the sake of 'titillation' as Thorpe put it. The extension from African to all men was made, of course, over a century ago: in a well-known letter to his wife in 1861, Thomas Henry Huxley, speaking of his lectures to working men, said "by next Friday evening they will all be convinced they are monkeys."[3] Huxley was only joking, perhaps, but today the joke has clearly turned a little sour. Authors and commentators should reflect on the words of William Lawrence, and think of their human responsibilities.

No-one was more acutely aware of his responsibilities as a scholar and author than Teilhard de Chardin. In this concluding chapter we wish to expound (mostly in his own words) his far-reaching theory of the positive nature of the evolutionary process, and in particu-lar of the positive role and significance of *Homo sapiens* in it. In earlier chapters we have already quoted from his best-known work, THE PHENOMENON OF MAN. Here we draw attention to writings composed some fifteen years after the larger work, written near the end of his

[1] Lawrence, W. (28a), p. 110.
[2] Lawrence, W. *Op. cit.*, Part II, p. 106.
[3] Huxley, T. H. (27), Vol. 1, p. 276.

life with a fine directness and clarity. They are published in English in the volumes entitled THE APPEARANCE OF MAN and THE FUTURE OF MAN.

Teilhard was poles removed from the noisy, over-emotionalised clamour of the popular press with its concentration on the here-and-now, on 'impact' and 'instant reaction'. As a scientist he viewed man *sub specie evolutionis*, and as a priest and mystic he viewed him *sub specie aeternitatis*. On both counts he saw much more in man, when viewed fully and objectively, than is possibly allowed for in the 'naked ape' concept. It is important to realize that the fact that we live in an evolved and evolving world is an insight only very recently (in historical terms) acquired by man, which accounts for much of the confusion about its implications. By most people its truth is ignored for all practical purposes—one of the merits of Morris's book is that attention has at least been focussed on the matter. Man's confusion over the popular exposition of evolution comes about from the anxiety and fear to which standard accounts give rise. Teilhard starts one of his last and most mature essays[1] with an analysis of the three principal fears to which inadequate understanding of the evolutionary process has given rise:

"First, the fear of being lost in a world so great and so full of indifferent or hostile beings that humanity seems positively to have no more importance in it.

"Secondly, the fear of being henceforth and for ever *reduced to immobility*—contained, as we are, in a zoological group so stabilized that even if the world were directed by nature towards some summit of consciousness, the biological exhaustion of our species would force us to renounce all hope of ever reaching that height.

"Lastly, fear of being *shut in*, imprisoned within an irremediably closed world, in which, even if it were not lost or arrested at present, humanity could not help striking tomorrow, when it reaches the peak of its trajectory, against an impassable barrier of reversibility which would force it to fall backwards.

[1] Teilhard de Chardin, P. (54). Omissions and minor modifications in translation are enclosed within [ ] brackets.

"Fear of not being able to make itself understood. Fear of no longer being able to move. Fear of not being able to get out . . ."[1]

Later, in his introductory statement, he continues:

"To cure his metaphysical dizziness, man once liked to consider himself as standing ontologically and spatially at the very heart of the Universe. Today we can reach the same result, more seriously and more fruitfully, by recognizing that, for man and from man onwards (not because of any marvellous properties in the human being, but by virtue of the fundamental and general structure of the evolutionary force), the world behaves towards its thinking elements with the preservative and accumulative care of a convergent system.

"This I shall try to show, as I feel it, divorced from all metaphysics and all supernatural belief in 'ends'.

"To this *neo-anthropocentrism of movement* (man no longer the centre, but an arrow shot towards the centre of the Universe in process of concentration) there cannot fail to be objections. To establish my thesis, I must in fact make three successive affirmations:

—of the *critical* nature of the stage of Reflection (first part)

—of the biological value of the Social stage (second part)

—of the capacity of the universe to sustain the process of hominisation and nourish it to the end (without prematurely weakening or becoming exhausted) (third part).

"And these three decisions, although well supported by a mass of facts [readily] grouped and clarified by them, may well appear at first sight non-scientific to many of my readers.

[1] *Op. cit.*, pp. 208-209.

"To our present world 'physics' (as Aristotle would have called it), man who, on account of his state of maximum organic arrangement and maximum psychic interiorisation, might normally pose as the structural keystone of the universe, is still treated as an accident or incident in nature.

"I simply ask those who would call my interpretation of the facts imaginative or poetic to show me (and I will then concur) a perspective which more completely and naturally integrates the extraordinary (and misunderstood) phenomenon of man in the framework of our biology and energetics."[1]

Teilhard's essay, of which we can here give only brief extracts, must be consulted directly to see how faithfully and meticulously he carries out his plan of exposition, and makes good the three affirmations required to establish his thesis. As in all of his mature writings, two in particular of his greatest scientific insights illuminate his analysis and conclusions. Firstly, he emphasizes how man has felt himself to be diminished successively by the science of the infinitely large (cosmology) and by the science of the infinitely small, where indeterminacy plays so large a role. But now we are just entering the period of what Teilhard refers to as the science of the infinitely complex. Analysis of even the most basic building blocks of living matter, such as the DNA molecule, shows them to be made up of the most bewilderingly complex and elegant forms. And yet they have been evolved from inorganic, i.e. lifeless, material. There is no addition of 'life-force', or 'soul' to be invoked. We are considering here simply the intrinsic powers of matter to organize itself in increasingly complex hierarchies of forms. It is these complexities which not only surround us but also *constitute* us. In us the arrangement has become so complex that it can even reflect upon and analyse itself. It is in acquiring understanding of this new science of the infinitely complex that man is offered the greatest challenge and the greatest hope for the future; included in the study must also be the spiritual dimensions in man.

It is here that Teilhard achieved his second, and very considerable insight into the phenomenon of evolution. He has defined it

[1] *Op. cit.*, pp. 209-210.

as "The Law of Complexity/Consciousness". This represents a statement about the natural potential, the natural behaviour, of matter when seen in terms of evolutionary space-time, which in time will be ranked with Newton's formulation of the General Law of Gravitation. Teilhard even speaks of the "gravity of complexity" which

"expresses itself in animated complexes by a tenacity of survival or, more exactly, by an evolutionary exuberance that everyone sees and acknowledges without sufficiently trying to find its roots."[1]

It is, therefore, in the stuff of the universe itself, when studied on the time-scale that evolution demands, that he sees this second form of gravity

"making preferential selections, rare and fragile though they are, of everything, from the atom to the vertebrate, that falls (that is to say rises) in the direction of a maximum centro-complexity."[2]

If we are to deal honestly with the facts as we know them we must incorporate this new gravitational force into our thinking, and learn how to advance with it instead of trying all the time to fight it by reducing ourselves to lower forms of complexity. Resistance to new ideas has been characteristic of civilization and is now no less prevalent in our science-based culture. Teilhard recognizes that

"from its beginnings, modern science has continuously developed under the too exclusive sign of entropy (that is to say of the wearing down and disintegration of the universe). It should now be time to recognize that, [operating at right angles, as it were . . .] to an irresistible [decay] of universal energy and conjointly with this [decay] a second and no less irresistible current exists, forcing this same energy, as it [decays], to make a long circuit into the increasingly complex, that is to say, at the same time, into the increasingly conscious. [. . .] *Axis of complexity/consciousness*, as I shall call it, usefully transposable, I repeat, into *axis of cephalisation* (or *cerebration*) after the appearance in nature of nervous systems."[3]

---

[1] *Op. cit.*, p. 214, f.n.
[2] *Op. cit.*, p. 215.
[3] *Op. cit.*, p. 215.

Without this insight man and nature become as meaningless as modern nihilism makes them out to be, the result merely of the play of chance. A reductionist approach to the study of evolution concludes that the 'pattern' is in fact a meaningless ramification of strands thrown up by chance. Teilhard was very conscious of what his scientific colleagues were saying, and saw how his conclusions, based on a fuller examination of a wider range of phenomena, would alter their picture:

"As set out in works of systematisation, the world of phyla (whether living or extinct) appears at first sight an impenetrable forest in which we have the justifiable impression that biologically we are lost. What place does our species occupy? Are there, indeed, even definable places in this disconcerting proliferation where every branch, every trunk appears to spring out at its own angle towards some success of a different type? By what right can we decide that, biologically speaking, a protozoan is less than a metazoan, or that a spider is not as perfect in its kind as a mammal? In short in the different expressions of life are not all things equal?

"This is what respected scholars, apparently for lack of sufficient reflexion on the 'law of complexity/consciousness', repeat all around us. And this is what we instinctively feel to be wrong. But only too often, fearful of appearing naively vain of our condition as men, we do not know how to answer them. As if we had not a very simple criterion or index to guide us and show us our place in the jungle of zoological forms—the very criterion that I have just pointed to when speaking of the world progress of corpusculation: I mean the relative development of nervous systems.

"Among higher living beings (as every student knows), the nervous system (studied in the most diverse phyla) shows the single perfectly clear tendency to gather cephalically into increasingly large ganglia. Whether insects or vertebrates, it is rare for a living group of any kind, provided one can follow it over a long enough space of time, not to show a notable advance in what we can call [either] *cephalisation* or *cerebration*. The global result of this has been to convince us that, from geological age to geological age, either in percentage or in absolute quantity, the mass of cerebralised matter has unceasingly increased (and this with increasing rapidity) within the biosphere.

"Scientists do not seem so far to have shown a particular interest in this general drift of living forms towards increasingly cephalised types. They merely call it simple evolutionary *parallelism*. And yet, even if one does not admit the identity just suggested between the 'axis of complexity/consciousness' and the 'zoological axis of cerebration'—still what a revelation!"[1]

Later in the essay Teilhard comments on man's place amongst the primates, and particularly on the origin of hominids from amongst the anthropoid group:

"I could not lay too much stress on the fundamental singularity of this group when it reaches maturity; that it represents on the living surface of the earth, the positively *polar* zone in which, after some two billion years of oscillation in all directions, the principal terrestrial axis of complexity/consciousness finally succeeded in fixing itself, before man's appearance, on the finally discovered path leading towards maximum cerebration.

"A zone essentially critical by nature, in which it is quite natural that an extraordinary event should very soon have occurred.

"One might say that in the space of only a million years (the last) the earth has grown a new skin. At the end of the Pliocene it was still entirely 'savage'—that is to say without the least trace of what we call civilization or culture. Today, on the other hand, wherever we go, man's presence in one form or another is impossible to avoid.

"To explain such a metamorphosis performed in so short a time, we must certainly assume that towards the beginning of the Quaternary a major event occurred in the realm of

[1] *Op. cit.*, pp. 219-220.

J

life; an event that palaeontology and prehistory have been pursuing for more than a hundred years, devoting the better part of their activities to the search. [. . .]

"Paradoxically, man who by his appearance has changed everything over the entire expanse of the continents, seems to have appeared almost without a notable change in the phylum on which he was grafted.

"Can it be that his much vaunted singularity is no more after all than an accident or an illusion? Can those scholars be right who still maintain that between hominians and anthropoids no 'natural' difference exists, only a difference of degree: man a wilier animal, perhaps, but from the biologist's point of view, just as much an animal as the others?"

(We might note in passing that this is the whole burden of the argument of THE NAKED APE).

"To meet this opinion, and supporting myself on all that I have said since the beginning of this study, I should like to show here the degree to which the hominisation of life [. . .] demands to be viewed by science as an evolutionary event of the first magnitude: always *provided* that the mental phenomenon called that 'of reflection' is first of all correctly defined in its psychic nature and justly appreciated in its physical reverberations.

Man, a reasoning animal', said Aristotle.

'Man, a reflective animal', let us say more exactly today, putting the accent on the evolutionary characteristics of a quality which signifies the passage from a still diffuse consciousness to one sufficiently well centred to be capable of coinciding with itself. Man not only 'a being who knows' but 'a being who knows he knows'. Possessing *consciousness raised to the power of two*, as has been said with perfect accuracy. Do we sufficiently feel the radical nature of the difference?

"Under the impact of this passage from simple to squared numbers, we all become aware that the entrance is open for the hominised consciousness into a new inner world: the world of the Universe *as thought.* [. . .]

"In some of the most learned books, they try to convince us that even taking into account his highest psychological faculties, man is no more than *unus inter pares* with the other animals: because, they assure us, the animals *also* are *intelligent* in their way. To this abuse of language I shall merely answer: Irresistibly—the whole history of hominisation proves it—intelligence (I mean here *true* intelligence— the intelligence that universalizes and foresees) tends to make the species possessing it coextensive with the earth. *In terms of function, reflexion planetises.* Under these conditions, how can one avoid seeing that, if one or another of the organic combinations realised by life had preceded man (as they allege) in attaining reflection, then there would have been no place left for man and man would never have appeared in nature? The animals may, justifiably, surprise us by the astonishingly diverse and direct varieties of their powers of cognition. But despite the amazing sagacity of their instinct, there is one thing that we can state *a priori* in every case: in none of them has this instinct ever succeeded in raising itself to the 'second power'. For if it had done so, from this focus (and not from the human mind) the Noosphere would immediately have been formed.

"Relying on this sufficiently weighty proof, we can be certain, absolutely certain, of this. By the sole fact of his entering into 'Thought', man represents something entirely singular and absolutely unique in the field of our experience. On a single planet, there could not be more than one centre of emergence for reflection."[1]

Then, in a few short questions Teilhard sums up the significance of this critical step in evolution:

[1] *Op. cit.*, pp. 222-225.

"In man, fantastically enough, the whole of evolution rebounds on itself. And at what speed? in what direction? and if the movement is driven to accelerate continuously, towards what form of emergence and fulfilment?"[1]

Biological and social evolution are, for Teilhard as for the present authors, in continuity with each other. But a critical change occurs with the advent of the noosphere:

"Correlatively with its change of motion this *New Evolution* has become capable of utilizing for its ends an equally *new* form of *heredity*, much more flexible and richer, without being any the less 'biological' on that account. It is no longer a matter only of combinations of chromosomes transmitted by fertilization, but *educative* transmission of a complex continuously modified and augmented by conduct and thought. Within and in virtue of this complex, individual human beings are so subtly developed through the centuries that it is strictly impermissible to compare any two men who are not contemporaries—that is to say are taken from two quite different times t and t^1 of the Noosphere.

"By what mysterious labour of groping and selection is it formed, this *additive and irreversible* kernel of institutions and viewpoints to which we adjust ourselves at birth and which we each contribute to enlarge, more or less consciously and infinitesimally, throughout our lives? What is it that makes one invention or idea among millions of others 'take on', grow and, finally, fix itself unchangeably as a human axiom or *consensus*? [. . .]

"*There are* technical discoveries (Fire, Nuclear Physics, etc.) and *there are* intellectual revelations (the rights of the individual, the reality of cosmogenesis, etc.), which once made or received are man's for ever [. . .] . . . a living force impregnating and completing, in its most essential humanity, each new fraction of human material as it newly appears.

[1] *Op. cit.*, p. 227.

"No, it is certainly untrue that, as is still said, the human being in us starts from zero with each new generation. [. . .]

"So it is principally by trying thoroughly to analyse the evolutionary possibilities and requirements of *our collect-ively thought* Universe (in which our thinking individualties ultimately find their continuity and consistency) that we can best hope ultimately to glimpse in broad outline the continuation and end of hominisation on earth."[1]

The dangers and difficulties of the future are then analysed, in this particular work, in terms of the three stages of man, namely *reflection, co-reflection* and what Teilhard called *ultra-* or *supra-reflection*. His development of ideas on the challenge that faces mankind today— a challenge of enquiry and discovery about himself and his potential— can perhaps be counted, in this essay, amongst the noblest statements ever written in defence of human dignity. A passage towards the end recapitulates the argument and indicates where it leads him:

"Since Galileo (as Freud remarked), in the eyes of science, man has continually lost, one after another, the privileges that had previously made him consider himself unique in the world. *Astronomically*, first of all when (like and with the earth) he was engulfed in the enormous anonymity of the stellar bodies; then *biologically*, when like every other animal he vanished in the crowd of his fellow-species; *psycho-logically*, last of all when an abyss of unconsciousness opened in the centre of his *I*; by three successive steps in four centuries, man, I repeat, has seemed definitely to redis-solve in the common ground of things.

"Now, paradoxically, this same man is in process of re-emerging from his return to the crucible, more than ever *at the head of nature;* since by his very melting back into the general current of convergent cosmogenesis, he is acquiring in our eyes the possibility and power of forming in the heart of space and time, *a single point of universalisation* for the very stuff of the world.

[1] *Op. cit.*, pp. 242-244.

"To universalise . . ."[1]

The theme here introduced is one that has attracted many of the world's thinkers with dreams of the unification of mankind in peace and co-operative endeavour. Because of shortcomings in logic and in scientific and philosophical method such theses are often easy to dismiss as utopian nonsense. We cannot do that with Teilhard, because his appeal to established scientific fact is unremitting and logically compelling, even when spiced with poetic simile and metaphor. After the initial rash enthusiasm that greeted his works, and the inevitable reaction that the enthusiasts provoked, there is now a steady 'build-up' of serious and concentrated studies of his ideas. The essay from which we have been quoting was one of the last he ever wrote. It concludes with a moving section on the 'personal universe' which he had come to recognize, and on the spiritual significance of the personal. We shall not expound his conclusions here, because the two authors of this book will not be expected, nor could they hope, to agree on the particular type of christian spirituality of which he writes so well. Yet they can agree that a spiritual goal is not only essential for man but is somehow inevitable, one that is bound in time to replace those typically 'bourgeois' attitudes characteristic of human aggressors, and of those 'naked apes' amongst us who believe in progress only at the material level. We conclude, therefore, with a quotation from another late essay by Teilhard with which we find ourselves in full agreement:

> "In the present age, what does most discredit to faith in progress (apart from our reticence and helplessness as we contemplate the 'end of the Race') is the unhappy tendency still prevailing amongst its adepts to distort everything that is most valid and noble in our newly-aroused expectation of an 'ultra-human', by reducing it to some form of threadbare millenium. The believers in progress think in terms of a Golden Age, a period of euphoria and abundance; and this, they give us to understand, is all that evolution has in store for us. It is right that our hearts should fail us at the thought of so 'bourgeois' a paradise.

"We need to remind ourselves yet again, so as to offset this

[1] *Op. cit.*, pp. 268-269.

truly pagan materialism and naturalism, that although the laws of biogenesis by their nature presuppose, and in fact bring about, an improvement in human living conditions, it is not *well-being* but a hunger for *more-being* which, of psychological necessity, can alone preserve the thinking earth from the *taedium vitae*. And this makes fully plain the importance of what I have already suggested, that it is upon its point (or superstructure) of spiritual concentration, and not on its basis (or infrastructure) of material arrangement, that the equilibrium of Mankind biologically depends."[1]

It is, perhaps, not too fanciful to see in some of the worldwide attitudes of youth today, with their wholesale rejection of the bourgeois values of the consumer-society (whether in western or eastern Europe or in the "third world") the first sign of an extensive growth of man towards *more-being* rather than simple *well-being*. It is more important to live than to have. Once that lesson is learned the fundamental inner drives of man might be channelled away from the naked aggression characteristic of naked apes, and into those realms of experience, in science and art, and exploration of all kinds, that are the birth-right of *Homo sapiens* if only he is prepared to live up to his name.

---

[1] Teilhard de Chardin, P. (53), p. 302-303.

Bibliography

1 Ardrey, Robert (1961), AFRICAN GENESIS, London: Collins

2 Ardrey, Robert (1967), THE TERRITORIAL IMPERATIVE, London: Collins

3 Bagehot, W. (1869), PHYSICS AND POLITICS, London

4 Barnett, S. A. (1967), INSTINCT AND INTELLIGENCE, London: MacGibbon & Kee

5 Benedict, Ruth (1942), RACE AND RACISM, London: Routledge

6 Berkowitz, L. (1962), AGGRESSION: A SOCIAL PSYCHOLOGICAL ANALYSIS, New York: McGraw Hill

7 Bernal, J. D. (1968), THE ORIGIN OF LIFE, London: Weidenfeld and Nicolson

8 Bierens de Haan (1946), ANIMAL PSYCHOLOGY, London: Hutchinson

9 Blough, D. S. and Blough, P. M. (1964), EXPERIMENTS IN LEARNING, New York: Holt, Reinhart & Winston

10 Brain, Russell (1961), 'Body, Brain, Mind and Soul' in THE HUMANIST FRAME, London: Allen & Unwin

11 Brown, J. A. C. (1961), FREUD AND THE POST-FREUDIANS, London: Penguin Books

12 Cassirer, E. (1944), AN ESSAY ON MAN, New Haven, Conn.: Yale U.P.

13 Childe, V. Gordon (1942), MAN MAKES HIMSELF, London: Watts

14 Dethier, V. G. and Stellar, E. (1964), ANIMAL BEHAVIOUR, New Jersey: Prentice Hall

15 Dobzhansky, T. (1962), MANKIND EVOLVING, New Haven, Conn.: Yale U.P.

16 Dobzhansky, T. (1967), THE BIOLOGY OF ULTIMATE CONCERN, New York: New American Library

17 Firth, R. (1951), ELEMENTS OF SOCIAL ORGANISATION, London: Watts

18 Freud, S. (1929), CIVILIZATION AND ITS DISCONTENTS, London: Hogarth Press

19 Fromm, Erich (1942), THE FEAR OF FREEDOM, London: Routledge

20 Glover, E. (1947), WAR, SADISM AND PACIFISM, London: Allen & Unwin

21 Harding, M. E. (1947), PSYCHIC ENERGY, New York: Pantheon Books

22 Horney, Karen (1946), OUR INNER CONFLICTS, London: Routledge

23 Huxley, Aldous (1949), APE AND ESSENCE, London: Chatto & Windus

24 Huxley, J. S. (1942), EVOLUTION, THE MODERN SYNTHESIS, London: Allen & Unwin

25 Huxley, J. S. (1942), THE UNIQUENESS OF MAN, London: Chatto & Windus

26 Huxley, J. S. (1961), THE HUMANIST FRAME, London: Allen & Unwin

27 Huxley, T. H. (1908), LIFE AND LETTERS, London: Macmillan

28 Klopfer, P. and Hailman, J. (1967), ANIMAL BEHAVIOUR, New Jersey: Prentice Hall

28a Lawrence, W. (1819) LECTURES ON PHYSIOLOGY, ZOOLOGY AND THE NATURAL HISTORY OF MAN, London.

29 Le Gros Clark, W. E. (1967), MAN-APES OR APE-MEN?, New York: Holt, Reinhart & Winston

30 Le Gros Clark, W. E. and Leakey, L. S. B. (1947), THE MIOCENE HOMINOIDEA OF EAST AFRICA. FOSSIL MAMMALS, London: British Museum of Natural History

31 Lorenz, Konrad (1966), ON AGGRESSION, London: Methuen

32 Macbeath, A. (1952), EXPERIMENTS IN LIVING, London: Macmillan

33 Mead, Margaret (1956), NEW LIVES FOR OLD, London: Gollancz

34 Medawar, P. B. (1960), THE FUTURE OF MAN. (Reith Lectures), London: Methuen

35 Montagu, Ashley (1957), THE DIRECTION OF HUMAN DEVELOPMENT, London: Watts

36 Morris, Desmond (1967), THE NAKED APE, London: Cape

37 Needham, Joseph (1937), INTEGRATIVE LEVELS. A REVALUATION OF THE IDEA OF PROGRESS. (Herbert Spencer Lecture), Oxford U.P.

38 Osman Hill, W. C. (1957), MAN AS AN ANIMAL, London: Hutchinson

39 Pannekoek, A. (1953), ANTHROPOGENESIS, Amsterdam: Holland Publishing Co

40 Pilbeam, D. R. (1967), MAN'S EARLIER ANCESTORS, Science Journal Vol. 3, 47-53

41 Pilbeam, D. R. and Simons, E. L. (1965), SOME PROBLEMS OF HOMINID CLASSIFICATION, Scientific American: Vol. 53

42 Popper, K. (1959), THE LOGIC OF SCIENTIFIC DISCOVERY, London: Hutchinson

43 Popper, K. (1963), CONJECTURES AND REFUTATIONS, London: Routledge

44 Russell, Bertrand (1948), AUTHORITY AND THE INDIVIDUAL (REITH LECTURES), London: Allen & Unwin

45 Ryle, Gilbert (1949), THE CONCEPT OF MIND, London: Hutchinson

46 Sellars, P. W. (1922), EVOLUTIONARY NATURALISM, London: Open Court Co

47 Sherrington, C. S. (1933), THE BRAIN AND ITS MECHANISM: Cambridge

48 Simons, E. L. (1965), NEW FOSSIL APES FROM EGYPT, Nature:
    Vol. 205

49 Spengler, Oswald (1931), DER MENSCH UND DIE TECHNIKE,
    Munich

50 Spengler, Oswald (1933), JAHRE DER ENTSCHEIDUNG, Munich

51 Storr, Anthony (1968), HUMAN AGGRESSION, London: Allen Lane,
    Penguin Press

52 Teilhard de Chardin, Pierre (1959), THE PHENOMENON OF MAN,
    London: Collins

53 Teilhard de Chardin, Pierre (1964), THE FUTURE OF MAN, London:
    Collins

54 Teilhard de Chardin, Pierre (1965), 'The Singularities of the
    Human Species' in THE APPEARANCE OF MAN, London: Collins

55 Thorpe, W. H. (1956), LEARNING AND INSTINCT IN ANIMALS,
    London: Methuen

56 Thorpe, W. H. (1962), BIOLOGY AND THE NATURE OF MAN,
    Oxford U.P.

57 Thorpe, W. H. (1965), SCIENCE, MAN AND MORALS, London:
    Methuen

58 Thorpe, W. H. (1968), THE SWARTHMORE LECTURE: QUAKERS AND
    HUMANISTS, London: Friends House Services Committee

59 Towers, Bernard (1968),'The Fetal And Neonatal Lung' in THE
    BIOLOGY OF GESTATION (ed. Assali), New York: Academic
    Press

60 Viaud, Gaston (1960), INTELLIGENCE, ITS EVOLUTION AND FORMS,
    London: Hutchinson

61 Waddington, C. H. (1961), THE NATURE OF LIFE, London:
    Allen & Unwin

62 White, L. A. (1949), THE SCIENCE OF CULTURE, New York: Farrar,
    Strauss

Index

Ardrey, Robert, xi, 22-24,
 29-33, 53, 57, 58, 63, 98, 99,
 101, 102
Aristotle, 71, 118, 122

Bagehot, W., 21
Barnett, S. A., 92
Benedict, Ruth, 105
Berkowitz, L., 107
Bernal, J. D., 23, 68
Blough, D. S., 92
Brain, Russell, 90
Broom, Robert, 31
Brown, J. A. C., 56, 64

Cassirer, E., 91
Childe, V. Gordon, 103
Le Gros Clark, W. E., 52, 78, 110

Dart, Raymond, 31
Darwin, Charles, 21, 41, 114
Davies, C. Colin, 108
Descartes, Rene, 70
Dethier, V. G., 97
Dobzhansky, T., 103-105

Firth, R., 99
Flugel, J. C., 106
Freud, Sigmund, 22, 30, 31,
 55-58, 64, 125
Fromm, Erich, 106

Glover, E., 57
Golding, William, xi
Goodall, Jane, 52
Guntrip, Harry, xi

de Haan, Bierens, 92
Hailman, J., 92
Haldane, J. B. S., 23

Harding, M. E., 64
Hobbes, Thomas, 24, 56
Holbrook, David, xi, 48
Horney, Karen, 64, 106
Huxley, Aldous, xv, 23
Huxley, Julian, 64, 75, 76, 79-81,
 86, 89, 97, 103
Huxley, T. H., 115

Klopfer, P., 92
Koestler, Arthur, 55
Kortlandt, Adrian, 52

Lawrence, D. H., 111
Lawrence, William, 114, 115
Leakey, L. S. B., 31, 78
Lorenz, Konrad, xii, 22, 24-30,
 33, 51, 54, 57-59, 61, 63, 106
Lotka, Alfred, 85

Macbeath, A., 99
Marx, Karl, 75, 103
Mead, Margaret, 100-101
Medawar, P. B., 85
Milne, Tom, 109
Molière, 62
Monboddo, James B., 115
Montagu, Ashley, 33, 54, 63, 91
Montagu, Ivor, 52, 58, 59
Morris, Desmond, xi, xv,
 xvi, xvii, xviii, xx, 22, 24, 26,
 31-33, 35-39, 41, 42, 46, 47,
 51-53, 57-59, 85, 98, 99, 101,
 114, 116

Needham, Joseph, 68
Newton, Isaac, 119

Osman Hill, W. C., 97

133